A Gypsy Dreaming in Jerusalem

Amoun Sleem

Edited by
Virginia McGee Butler

Amoun Sleem modeling clothing made by Dom women at the
Community Center, 2012.

© 2014

Published in the United States by Nurturing Faith Inc., Macon GA, www.nurturingfaith.net.

Library of Congress Cataloging-in-Publication Data is available.

978-1-938514-50-0

DEDICATION

This book is a gift to my father, Yasser Sleem, who taught me to live in peace but know when I needed to take a stand, encouraged me to have strength and confidence in myself, and gave me pride in the wonderful culture of Gypsy people.

CONTENTS

ENDORSEMENTS

Every person's life story is worth telling, but every once in a while there comes someone whose life story will move the masses. That's Amoun Sleem.
—Brittany Strange, friend and supporter of the Domari Society

Amoun and Domari are proof that miracles can still happen in Jerusalem. Against all odds, she is able to become teacher, leader, mentor. Without the benefit of any female leadership role model she invented a unique path and walked it with courage. She pays the highest price for her struggle for her people—she is usually alone on the front lines. Amoun's spirit is a force of nature. She has not succumbed to pressures from all sides "to be normal," bend her head, and accept a marginal role. Amoun can't help following her vocation to lift her people from the bottom strata of Jerusalem society. Amoun is one of the bravest people I know. As long as there are Miracles like her in the world one can believe that leadership is a divine gift.
—Anat Hoffman
Chairperson, the Domari Society of Gypsies in Jerusalem

I'm thrilled that Amoun's story is finally being told. You'll be amazed, shocked, awed and inspired by this courageous and very special woman. Thanks to her stamina and vision, other Dom women and their precious children are now able to have a future!"
—Petra van der Zande, friend and supporter of Amoun and the Domari Center in Jerusalem

Our acquaintanceship started now almost 3 years ago, on a warm day in October, when I entered the Domari Community Center for the first time. Long black hair, dark and fiery eyes and tall, already on the first sight a very special Arabic woman.

Happily laughing, she met us in the courtyard. "Ahlan wa sachlan," she greeted us and immediately disappeared to make us tea. I already felt very comfortable in the Center.

Amoun is a Dom woman. I soon learned: The Dom are not Arabs, they are Gypsies. As a minority they live in between Israeli and Arab people. At one point, Amoun could not bear the humiliation and discrimination of her people anymore and decided to do something.

Today she is the director of the Domari Society, which takes care of the Gypsies in Israel and Palastine. Also she is leading the first center for Gypsies in the Near East and this already for the last 10 years.

The way was not always easy. As a young girl she lived on the street and sold post cards. She herself refers to this period as her golden years. She learned a lot from the life on the street. At that time, she only knew a couple of words of English. She learned to be a business woman. Today she has graduated in economics and hotel management.

By now, we shared many ups and downs and it has always been a blessing to know her. I learned so much from her. The most important thing is to never give up. Amoun never gives up. She also is a person who is able to take other people as they are. That is why everybody feels comfortable at the Domari Community Center.

—Stephanie Gauger, friend and supporter of the Domari Society

Amoun Sleem's life story is unusual, fascinating and inspirational. She has overcome countless obstacles to express herself personally, and in representation of the Dom Gypsy community in Israel and the Palestinian Territory. Her stories speak to the struggles and triumphs of a rich cultural heritage threatened by social and political struggles, and vibrantly convey one woman's daring determination to be heard.

—Ariela 'Mouna' Marshall, friend and former volunteer at
Domari Community Center, human rights advocate

Amoun Sleem's life story is an inspiring true tale of personal resilience and strength in the face of incredible odds: poverty, bigotry, misogyny, lack of educational opportunities, and the weight of history. But it is also the remarkable story of a misunderstood people whose language, culture, and history deserve to survive, and the woman who refused to let it die. Having spent a year working at the Domari Community Center, I can attest that Amoun changes lives — not only of those Dom people who come to the Center to find education and community, but the lives of everyone lucky enough to get involved with her noble project.

—Rena N. Lauer, medieval historian, worked at the Domari Community
Center as a Shatil/NIF Social Justice Fellow (2005-6)

I love Amoun! And I fully support her mission to present and preserve the beauty and strength of Gypsy (Dom) children, women and men in Jerusalem.

East-Jerusalem has been my home away from home ever since I traveled to the Middle East for the first time in 1989. It took me, however, a good 10 years before I met Amoun. She showed me the life and plight of her community, living nearby Saint Anne's tomb and Lion's gate.

I had the privilege to support her with some funds and advice and am astonished by what she has achieved since: using her talents and energy as well as her humor and brains.

Please, take some time to get to know Amoun and through her the colorful and energetic Domari Society if Gypsies in Jerusalem. You won't regret it!

—Lilian Peters, friend of Amoun

Amoun's bravery is astounding. As a Dom woman in the Middle East, her stories capture a unique perspective very few can provide, and I've fallen in love with her and this beautiful community through her stories.

—Michael R. Yates, friend and former volunteer worker
at the Community Center

INTRODUCTION

When I was a child selling postcards to tourists, I never thought I would write a book. Being raised in the Gypsy culture was like a movie with sweet parts mixed with painful times. In my childlike thinking, I had no idea how that drama would continue or how it would end. Looking back to the change from that childhood to becoming Director of the Domari Center gave me an incentive to tell my story and show the world what it is like to be a Gypsy woman.

As I tell my story, this drama makes me laugh and cry. It was easy to learn that I was Gypsy, but it was not easy being Gypsy. In those days and even now, the world around me shows the feeling, "You have no right to live because you are Gypsy." Those are moments for crying.

Sometimes I feel my oil is finished. I'm tired of Gypsy ways. I feel like I'm holding water, not taking it to the house. I blame God for choosing to make me Gypsy. This is only at moments, but I live in reality and deal with it. I try to be confident, tell people who I am even using the negative word "Nawar" for myself. I'm dealing with it and moving into the future. As a young child, I didn't think so much about it, but as a teenager and adult I think about it. I've always had to keep my expectations low because nothing comes smoothly. In the sixth class when I went back to school, I decided this all needs to change.

Then I remember great moments with my dear family. I remember people who were my champions and helped me make my way. Those are the moments for smiles. Every day of my life comes with steps. On those steps are those who would push me down and others who would help me up.

I thank God that my life was never boring. Every day had a story—a funny story or a painful story. In this good life, I call myself "Survivor" because my will is strong and helps me prepare for each new day. I plan what to do and how to do it in a way that will not bring pain.

I write this book to show the difficulties of being Gypsy, but also to show the creativity and beauty in the Gypsy culture. I write it to thank the people who were placed in my life as helpers and encouragers. Many of them have passed away. I hope the readers will enjoy my story as I have enjoyed living it. I give thanks to God for what He has given me in these years.

CHAPTER ONE

At Home in Jerusalem

Nighttime came, but not sleep. How could we go to sleep with so many visitors? I remember my home as a center for the Gypsy people. They liked to come and drink tea and eat at my home. My father Yasser and my grandmother Amar were very generous and liked to give to people. The guests were Dom or other neighbors. They came and stayed late, talking and watching TV. I remember when my father came with the TV. It was like a wedding, and everybody was happy.

My parents, my five brothers and three sisters, and I lived in one big room in a house. This room had everything in one. My grandmother had her own small room where one of my brothers or one of my sisters would sleep with her. In the large room there was the small black-and-white TV and a large closet for everyone to use. Not until the end of the 90s did we get a new room for the girls and a small living room. My sister Zarifeh saved the money from her work to build these rooms.

In the evening, we always had a wood fire so we could cook. We cooked inside. There was a small round table for guests and for my dad only.

Amoun making yogurt.

For a family meal, we had a strange style of eating, which we still have to this moment. We sat in a circle on the ground with the food on a big metal tray in the middle. In my father's style, he liked to see us around him—and he liked to control us, to be sure that we were eating what he offered us. I still prefer to sit on the floor to eat, spreading a place before me on the rug.

These were joyful peaceful moments except when we had turkey meat, which I never liked at all. My brothers and sisters were 50/50 about the turkey. I had to play all kinds of tricks not to eat my piece and to hide it from my father's eyes. In the end, I ran outside and gave it to the dog. I kept doing this until the day he discovered my trick. I got a great punishment that day.

My grandmother, my hero, saved me. She said, "Leave her," and "It's okay."

From that day, I never liked turkey meat. I can't eat it at all. But when I see turkey, I remember my dad and his vision about us eating. He wanted us to eat what God presented us that day because we were just a simple family. We needed to appreciate any kind of food that was offered.

We would sit around the fire to make us warm and ready to sleep. Finally, the talkers would go away. I felt safe in the night as all of us lay down together. I never felt like it was crowded. The room felt great, and there was safety next to my brothers and sisters.

The dirt floor had many pits. My grandmother made a smooth mattress from old clothes and other different fillings. I don't have any idea what they were. I liked the different colors. The mattress was beautifully handmade with designs like flowers. If the mattress felt thin when we started to sleep, it was painful, and we could not get comfortable. Sometimes the rough floor gave us back pain, and we did not sleep well. The next morning when we woke up, we were still tired. It felt like one eye was bigger than the other. Still, we were happy, and I was so glad to be among my brothers and sisters.

We children even found ways to have fun with the problems in the house. There were holes and pockets in the very bad dirt floor. We used to hide things in them—not really bad things, maybe sweets that we were not allowed to eat.

Sometimes we made up a game to play with marbles in a hole. The players would try to shoot their marbles into the hole. The one who got the most marbles in the hole won them all. We kept them in a sock. When my grandmother got mad about having them everywhere, she would throw them out into the cobblestone street.

I would sometimes find small things in a hole—maybe my father lost a small coin or my grandmother lost beads from her clothes or her fancy headdress. I never thought about how we were living unless I invited a friend to visit. Then I felt shy and wondered where I could entertain them when I didn't have my own room. Mostly, I remember that my childhood was rich.

CHAPTER TWO

At Home with My Gypsy People

I belong to the Dom people in the Old City of Jerusalem. History says our people came out of India more than 1,000 years ago. Some people mistakenly believed we came out of Egypt and called us Gypsies. The terms "Dom" or "Gypsy" mean the same. "Nawar" is a derogatory word used by people who are prejudiced against the Dom. I like the term "Gypsy" because it brings to my mind the history of romance and creativity associated with my people. Like any community, Gypsies have their own special lifestyle. They like to live close to each other and have stayed in the same basic area for many years.

I heard stories from my family about our past. Records kept by the Gypsy leader show that we are among the oldest people groups who now live in Jerusalem. My family has documents showing that we have been here at least since 1920. Other stories are passed down orally by family members.

My father told me about the years gone by that we thought of as the Golden Years. He said our people earned their living making things with their hands—like weaving reed mats. Some were tinkers. Some played music, sang, and danced. Others made sieves, drums, and birdcages.

Amoun Sleem standing in the yard of her home beside the
Old City Wall of Jerusalem, 2013.

The Dom entertained with their trained animals. They loved animals—especially horses—and treated them like children.

Many years ago, the Dom lived in a good place in the Wadi Goss in Jerusalem. The land in that area belonged to an Arab man. When he decided to leave and sell his land, he offered to let my grandfather buy the land. At that time, the land was nothing, but now it is some of the most expensive land around Jerusalem. But my grandfather had some people living with him, and he thought he needed to save his money to care for his guests. The story still makes me sad. Perhaps if he had been able to buy the land, many things would be different for the Gypsies today.

Our home is near the Lions' Gate in Jerusalem. This leads to the entrance of the Via Dolorosa, a big attraction for tourists who come to walk the path Jesus walked during the last hours of his life. The gate's name comes from two sets of lions facing each other high on the wall of the gate. Suleiman the Magnificent dreamed lions would tear him apart unless he built a wall around Jerusalem so he built the wall quickly and had lions carved into it. Some people say they are leopards rather than lions, but I never look up to see them. I look at the metal part of the gate. When I see it, I know I'm almost home. The area has changed over the years. There used to be more hills, stone, and dirt. I miss the dirt.

In my childhood, people could look down inside our house from the top of the wall of the Old City in Jerusalem. Today we have a little more privacy. We often climbed from my house over the wall. Most of the time, I didn't think about how poor we were. I was pleased with the living love of my family and liked living in our house. I felt we had enough. Maybe I was too young to think big in those days.

From the time I was born and grew up in this family, wherever my eyes turned left or right, I saw bamboo trees surrounding that little garden that we had at our house in the Old City. I felt like God decorated that simple house with bamboo. When I say, "O, my God, it's beautiful trees," I really mean it in my heart. They are history with my family. They have been here over two hundred years to this moment. Sometimes when it is dry, we use pieces of the wood to put around flowers in our home.

Sometimes many Gypsies visited us from Palestine, Jordan, and abroad. Many were musicians and were professional at making the nay (reed flute). They were careful to cut a small piece of the bamboo to make a flute so they did not damage the trees. When they were finished making the flute, I was amazed at what beautiful music came out of it.

This bamboo was like a kid to my father and grandmothers. They were angry with anyone from the area who would cut it or damage it. The tree is like part of the family, and Arab people in the neighborhood attack it as if they were attacking us personally. Many times they burned

Olive trees and bamboo inside the Old City Wall of Jerusalem beside the Sleems' home, 2013.

our bamboo out of jealousy, and I thought it would never grow back. But by God's will, the bamboo grew stronger, more green, and more beautiful. It's like a message for the people who are jealous of our home, "We will be here. We are the walls surrounding Family Sleem."

This home has always been very important to my family. At the end of the 70s and the beginning of the 80s, my grandmother had Jewish settlers that wanted to buy her house. They kept coming. She kept refusing. They would say, "We can give you a nice house, a good check."

The house had no toilet inside. My grandmother liked to sit under a fig tree opposite the outside toilet. The settlers tried another method to make us move by shooting in the air. She was afraid and ran and locked herself in the toilet. Then they locked her in from the outside. She was yelling, "Go away."

The neighbors saw and should have called the police, but they were watching a movie. They waited for the end of their program, but the police heard the shots and came quickly.

My grandmother tore the toilet down because she didn't want the reminder of that day. She didn't talk to the neighbors for a couple of years. She thought they should have remembered the saying, "A close neighbor is better than a faraway brother."

It is hard to write the next part, but I want to be honest in this book and mention all parts of my life, even the bad and difficult parts.

Our house for more than two hundred years passed from grandfather to grandfather even with problems facing us. People bothered us, threw stones, burned our bamboo, and threw garbage in front of the doors. They asked, "Why does a Gypsy family have such a house?"

We promised our dad, and that was his father's last wish before he died, that we would keep this place until we die. He taught us to be patient, not to fight back, just to pray to God to protect us, to protect our children, and to protect the family in this house.

This sweet small house in the Old City is my connection with my home. I love it and care about it. I would not change it for a big castle. I'm confident with each piece of wood and stone in this house. We have had the most difficult and happy moments that we've lived in this place. We're happy fixing every small piece of this place to look like a normal house. I hope God will bless this Family Sleem in this place to bring the message of love for home to the kids living here now so they may keep it for their children in the future.

Dom camp outside the Old City Walls, photo used with the permission of Ecole Biblique, Jerusalem.

Dom carrying water pots outside the Old City Walls, photo used with the permission of Ecole Biblique, Jerusalem.

Dom women dancing outside the Old City Walls, photo used with the permission of Ecole Biblique, Jerusalem.

Dom camp outside the Old City Walls, men preparing lamb, photo used with the permission of Ecole Biblique, Jerusalem.

CHAPTER THREE

The Old City, My Playground

My preschool life was one of the most wonderful times with the presence of friends playing in the beautiful places of the Old City. No one stopped us from playing there. The world was simple, and we knew no hatred. We didn't think about the future and reflected only on what existed.

I had a favorite place in my life like a second home. The place was called the Church of St. Anne's and was near the Lions' Gate. I loved to be in this place. Always when I felt sad or wanted to cry, I found privacy here. I saw myself as the queen of the beauty and splendor of this place with great power. The place had great history.

The church is built on the site of a grotto believed by the Crusaders to be the birthplace of the Virgin Mary and is dedicated to Anna and Joachim. According to tradition, they were her parents, and she was born here. The French government owns the church. It is administered by the White Fathers, a Catholic order named for the color of their robes. It is near the Bethesda Pool, believed to be the place Jesus healed a paralyzed man. I just had a great feeling to sit here.

I sometimes drove the father of the church crazy, but not in a bad way. He was one of the White Fathers from France and ran behind me from place to place. It was a sport from morning to evening, and I think he liked what I was doing.

I loved to go fishing. In the garden of the church, there was a small pool. They put fish in there only for decoration. But this Gypsy girl decided the beautiful fish with the unusual colors were for catching, so I must find a way to do that. I found a recycled plastic basket used for drilling that someone had put beside the tree. I took the basket and began my fishing. The father saw me from the window. This tall thin man ran like crazy in his white robe, his brown belt swinging, and his eight-inch wooden cross going back and forth like windshield wipers. Of course, he would not shout. He caught me and hit me on my bottom. He said, "Hapsoukay!" I don't know what that means.

Only a few people had this special tree called "shami," a deep red mulberry tree, but my family had one for a long time planted by our house. My grandmother made the berries into jam to use on bread in the morning. Many Gypsies used the tasty juice for a wedding. They mixed water and the flower juice together to make it rich.

I had something else in mind for the fruit. When you touch the ripe fruit, your hands turn red. From far away, people see it as blood. I painted my face and hands from the berries until I looked like a red balloon.

I put it on my body and went to the church to show the Father how I looked. "I need your help," I said and pretended to be crying.

The poor Father left everything in his hands and came to help me. He brought me his first aid box and started to clean up my hands. He cleaned and cleaned, but there was nothing hurt or cut.

When he seemed to be getting angry, I thought of running away. Instead, I put on my sweet face. I said to myself that it was April First when small white lies were allowed.

He stood me on my legs and spanked me on the bottom to teach me a lesson. Then I really cried and cried. His sweet heart smiled and said, "Hapsoukay!"

St. Anne's Church is known for its wonderful acoustics. Many groups come here to sing. I especially liked the African groups. They sang hallelujahs with enthusiasm and used swaying and arm movements. I thought I would help them by joining in. Then I sang "Hallelujah" during one of their silences. The father pulled me by the ear and escorted me from the church. That ear may still be longer than the other.

The pastor was one of the finest people. I called him, "Abuna," a respectful name meaning pastor. Our beautiful friendship, tender and based on tolerance, sometimes became quarrelsome depending on what I was doing that day. At hard times, I went to the pastor. In later years, when he died, I grieved for my good friend.

My second favorite place was the Jerusalem Wall. At that age, I did not know the history of the place. In the wall were some small windows. When I wanted to run outside, I would squeeze through them.

I felt like the old fiction of Vassoaa, sometimes called Amoura, in one of my grandmother's Gypsy bedtime stories. She came from the clouds and made your dreams come true if you were a good person and brought punishment if you were bad. She might be beautiful, or she might come like an animal, or like something scary. Sometimes you might hear people say, "You're acting like Amoura," if you were acting crazy.

I was a human being living in poverty, but here I could look up to the Mount of Olives. In the autumn there was a beautiful red flower blooming outside the walls of Jerusalem. I felt like a princess who had everything.

When I felt a kind of sadness, I came here to talk to God. The hill where the cemetery is outside the city walls looked so high to me as a child. Looking up at the hill, it was like a mountain to me, and God was far up on the mountain. The place made me dream and gave me a feeling of contentment.

CHAPTER FOUR

My Open-Handed Mother

I think a mother is the most important creature on earth for any living being. My mother was a beautiful woman from a simple family. Her father was Egyptian from Cairo, and her mother was a Gypsy from Jordan. His family did not like that he married a Gypsy woman. Because of the marriage, his brothers did not want him to return to Cairo so he moved to Jordan. By Gypsy tradition, we count our family roots as coming from the father, so my mother was considered Egyptian. We had little contact with her family.

My father and mother met in Jordan. This was at a time that the Gypsy people would travel from their homes to go to Jordan, Iraq, Syria, Lebanon, Saudi, and Kuwait for work. They traded and sold things—animals, carpets, metals, and other second-hand things. They would travel for a few weeks at a time and live in tents, but they returned to their stone houses in Jerusalem. People in those countries would wait for their visit to trade with them. They would travel by foot or on horses or donkeys. My dad's family traveled to Jordan and there met my mother's family. Yasser and Miriam met several times when their families visited. When they were thirteen or fourteen years

Miriam, Amoun's mother (seated); Amar, Amoun's sister (standing).

old the families arranged the marriage and my parents agreed. They were married in Jordan and all the Gypsy community was invited. This was in the area called *Al Hashmeh Ashemaleh*. A large Gypsy community is still there including the Al Masri family, my mother's family. After the wedding my mother returned to Jerusalem with my father. The marriage with my father was arranged, but he liked her. Some of us look like her.

Her philosophy was, "What is in my hand does not belong to me." She used to go to the Old City market, called

The Butcher's Market. It ran from the Damascus Gate to the Church of the Holy Sepulcher. They sold meat, vegetables, fruits, and other items. My father gave her money for buying the food. She took two plastic baskets, green for fruits and vegetables and red for meat. She brought them home with the baskets on her head. She would meet one person and then another. Each time she gave them a banana or an apple. When she got home, half the food was gone. My father was angry.

She went to the market every three days. I liked to go with her. Sometimes we crossed the mosque, called Dome of the Rock, in a shortcut. She would also give the guards a piece of fruit. Near one gate of the mosque is the African community. There was a girl there who would pull my hair or hit me when I was alone. So I hurried across going and coming so she couldn't catch me.

I shall never forget one small memory of my mother. When I went to kindergarten, they had a party for us. I had no good clothes. I told my mom, "I need a dress." I cried and cried.

She told me she would get it for me, but it was evening. Most of the shops were closed, and I needed it in the morning. I cried again. I didn't think whether she had the money to get the dress. She asked for money from the family and from our neighbors. I don't know how, but she got it. She took me that evening and hurried to reach the shops before it was too late. She went from shop to shop to find a good price with the little money she had.

She bought me treats and said, "You'll be so beautiful at the party." I dressed up in my long black dress. She fixed my hair. I was so proud of my mother.

That day I learned a lesson. She didn't have that much in a life filled with care and pain, but she was always ready for her family. She kept her promise to me. How could I forget her or go one day without thinking of her. I take her as my white angel and try to give to others like she gave to me.

We had a simple house, but every corner had a beautiful side. With stones and small plants here and there, the house was like a piece of art. My mother was generous in giving to her plants. It made our home look nice. In the meantime, it also taught us to live with nature and make the impossible possible.

In the stones around our house, my mother made a small round place to grow plants by the entrance. She planted mint there, and in another one, she planted basil. It was a mark for the Family Sleem. All the neighbors cut from this mint. It just grew bigger and bigger. This plant meant so much to her, she took care of it like her own body.

Everyone asked my mom what was the secret of the nana (mint) at your house. She said, "I just treat it like one of my children. I know in the morning I have to feed my child so I feed it and give it water." The water was scarce at the time. We had to buy it because we didn't have our own tap. For many years, my mother cut the mint and gave it to the whole neighborhood.

We say our tea was the best in the neighborhood. All the neighbors enjoyed drinking tea in our house. It's like a secret recipe that nobody knows what's behind it. My mom and my grandmother used to make the tea, and the magic continues with my sister Amar. Every guest who enters this home enjoys that cup of tea at Family Sleem.

One of the most beautiful things I remember about my mom is her love for an olive tree and her emotional attachment to every leaf of that tree. The tree grew beside the wall around the Old City. She thought the tree was a blessing for the Holy Land. She liked the shade. She would say, "This tree is like a mother. It gives so much but asks so little. The tree gives fruit, oil, shade, and decoration, but receives only a little water to keep going until she grows old."

My mother prepared her own olives in many different ways. She fixed them with very beautiful sweet and hot peppers. She made the olives just with olive oil or black olives with salt and oil. She learned from my grandmothers to make her own olive oil soap.

Tourist group from the USA having tea and refreshments at the Sleems' home
in the Old City.

When my mother died, we planted an olive tree on her grave as our gift for her. All of my brothers and sisters, along with my father and grand-mothers went to the cemetery to plant the tree. Today, that tree is one of the biggest olive trees in the cemetery above the garden tomb. The tree still gives olives and shows us the story of my mother—that she was a giving person. The tree stays green and covers my mother's grave with shade.

My mother died when I was seven. Loss of my mom at a young age cost me a lot as I got older. She left a family of nine children. My feelings about this loss were too difficult to reveal to anyone, so I locked them up for many years. I only cried to God in anger. I shouted, "I need my mom. I need a chest full of love. I want that kind person." I don't have many memories of her, but I love and miss her and always think about her. I hold onto small memories of her that will live inside me until I die.

In the Gypsy community, men are expected to remarry when a wife dies. However, my father decided when to follow customs and when to disregard them. He did not remarry. My grandmother helped my father with all the children until she died three years after my mother.

CHAPTER FIVE

My Dad Becoming
Father and Mother

The death of my mother left my father responsible for the family. I hated when he took me shopping for clothes! My father had a man's taste, and he bought me outfits that looked like a little boy—always T-shirts and jeans. I had to wear T-shirts with horrible prints. He was not democratic, and it did no good to complain. I should take whatever he bought me. Of course, I went home with a long face, hiding my tears inside my eyes. I couldn't show him I didn't like these clothes, but the neighborhood girls looked much better than me in their fashions.

But I loved it when he bought me shoes. He was good with shoes and bought the best of high quality leather. Sometimes from my happiness with the shoes, I laid them under my pillow and dreamed about the beautiful shoes of Cinderella. My father only had good taste in shoes and bad taste in clothes.

In those moments, I wished my mother was alive and could buy me clothes like the other girls. I remembered her promise of the dress when I

Yasser, Amoun's father.

was in kindergarten and what she did to get it for me. I still have a problem with clothes. I have a different taste, and it takes time to be confident with what I buy.

I remember a beautiful place where I used to go with my dad and some of my brothers. We went to the vegetable market in Ramallah. My dad bought enough fresh vegetables, eggs, fruit, and meat for my family for one week. I loved watching him argue about the prices. I think he had a reason to take me every time. He wanted me to learn how to deal with the market and its people.

I loved the way he chose the potatoes. He looked like a chef, choosing the best vegetables for his kitchen. He was always fair with the prices and was kind and respectful to everybody. Most of the people knew him in the market because he came every week. They loved him because he made jokes with the sellers and gave a nice atmosphere to the market. People called him man and wife because he had no wife and came every week to buy vegetables for his family.

I stood beside him holding the bags. They became heavier and heavier. My face looked sad. I thought, "Let's go. We are finished," but I could not complain.

I think it was kind of his fantasy to go to the market and shop, but for a teenager like me, it became boring after a short time. In the end, my father had his reasons for taking me. Now I realize he was right and put us on the right way to know how to survive. Now I can go to any market and am able to make good choices.

At the end of the market trip, my father loved to give us a treat. The treat was to go to his friend's place in a Bedouin tent. The friend made the best kebab and meat on the barbecue with good humus and the best pita bread. My father entered the place, and the man hugged him. He gave us the best place in the corner of the tent where we could sit and eat as a family together and enjoy our meal.

The man would have a short talk with my father—man talk about how life is going. After the meal, we would take a ride back to Jerusalem with a taxi full of many vegetables.

In every country, there is a Mother's Day. In the Family Sleem, we just switched this to Father's Day. We were happy shopping for my dad and finding simple, funny gifts. It depended on our income in those times. My poor dad got socks from me every year since that was the amount of money

I could afford. I kept buying socks for my dad in different colors, and he was glad that we remembered him on Mother's Day.

In school, there was a special meeting for mothers. My father showed up among many women from the school. He sat there without words, embarrassed that he was the only man with all those women. In the end, the teacher saw his face growing all kinds of colors. She started with my dad so he could be released in the beginning.

This great father, Yasser, went to many stations of life with us. We were proud to have such a father who was a mother and a father at the same time. I will always remember his kind heart and his patience with us, even though we had so many moments when we were naughty and not listening.

I appreciate what my father did at that time. He was trying to be a dad and a mother at the same time. He was trying to make us happy as much as he could with limited means.

CHAPTER SIX

Overcoming Hard Times

My father said my grandfather, Shaker Ibrahim, had a horse that he took everywhere he went. Before he ate, he put food out for the horse. Within two weeks of my grandfather's death, the horse died, too. I believe the horse must have missed him.

My family also liked to raise sheep. One of my uncles loved to raise white sheep with a lot of hair—only white sheep, really white. This man had a cleaning sickness. He had one sheep that he cleaned daily and taught him. He put a silver bell around his neck. Wherever my uncle went, the sheep went behind him, like a son. They called my uncle "Abu Haroof" – Father Sheep. Sometimes my uncle put him in our garden. After an hour or two of eating, the sheep would go home by himself. He knew where he was raised.

My uncle was a good-hearted man for animals. People said he had golden hands. His sheep looked wonderful, and people said if he entered them in a contest, they would win. I call these my golden days, when every day had a beautiful story like the sheep and my uncle talking about the sheep as if it were his son. We say Gypsies are full of imagined stories because their own story is like imagining. They love animals. They love nature. They love music. And they enjoy the simple life.

We had dogs and sometimes birds for pets. My grandmother liked to have chickens for eggs and to eat. You could smell the eggs she cooked with olive oil from far away.

My family liked to have the dogs we raised around the home. It was not popular with the Arab families in the neighborhood to have dogs, but my father and oldest brother Shaker enjoyed them. We have beautiful memories of two dogs in particular.

One dog was Jennie. She always stayed in front of the house or walked around the house. When my mother died, this dog followed us to the cemetery and cried like a human being. We realized that she was missing my mom like the rest of us.

Jennie was a female. One day she brought us seven nice puppies. We were glad, and my father decided to keep them. In the night, the dogs barked and barked. One of our neighbors called someone to come and poison the puppies and their mother. The next morning all of us children woke up with chicken pox and saw the added disaster with our puppies. My father was angrier at our neighbor than I have ever seen him.

Times were bad for Gypsies during the Six Day War. The Dom are a peace-loving people. They don't think about power and promoting themselves. In Israel, like much of the Middle East, the Gypsies are ignored. They are neither part of the Jewish State of Israel, nor are they accepted as part of the surrounding Arab communities. Because they are not influential outside their community, they don't involve themselves in wars and political fighting. Still their numbers dwindle. Some have left Israel during the conflicts to go to other places in the Middle East—Iraq, Iran, Syria, Libya, Turkey, and Egypt. In these days, many believe that their lives are tied to living and dying in Jerusalem. They have begun to believe they must stand up for their place and protect their homes. This is a change from the time when Gypsies were nomadic.

During the war, my family and other Gypsies fled to the nearby Church of St. Anne, just inside the Lions' Gate in Old Jerusalem, and stayed there. Those were days of worry and sadness. Many people were killed with no regard for whether they were children or adults, men or women. I felt such sadness when I heard the stories of the sufferings of my people during those times. Some described the war as being like "days in hell."

Poor people had no food and no way to get any. At night, they heard shooting and fighting. No one was allowed out on the streets.

The church and the sisters gave people food and a place to stay. They provided dried milk for the children. This was very important for my father with our nine very young children. The sisters shared their love for the people and helped them forget their problems. Still, those six days seemed like six years for my community.

One day my grandmother jumped from the wall of St. Anne's church and ran to our house to get food and flour to make bread for the Gypsies inside the church. While she was away, a missile fell on the church. My grandmother didn't know if her family was safe. She began to cry and sob loudly.

One of my uncles saw her and called, "Don't worry. We are all okay. Hurry, come inside." We thanked God that no one was killed.

Every day my grandmother made her way to our house to be sure no one broke in and robbed us. She knew robbers were taking things from many of the houses. The Gypsies were fortunate to have a strong person like my grandmother to help them through these hard days.

One or two years after Jennie and our puppies were poisoned, my father and my brother Shaker brought a German Shepherd to our home. He was a nice, young puppy that we named Jimmy. Shaker took care of him and tried to teach him. The dog would care for the family if strangers came nearby, but other times he was lazy. He just ate and slept.

During the First Intifada, on a Friday, there was so much trouble in our neighborhood. Soldiers were shooting rubber bullets, and there was a lot of gas. My father thought Jimmy would be hurt outside and decided to put him in his house. One soldier on the wall saw my father go outside into the yard and around the house. He thought that my father would send the dog after him. The soldier shot my father with a rubber bullet, which hit him in the lip. He was really lucky that he was not killed. Then Jimmy tried to attack the soldier, but one of my brothers controlled the dog while Shaker cared for my father. Jimmy made it through the Intifada and lived a long life. When he died, we felt like we shouldn't get a new dog because it would bring difficulty in the neighborhood with people who disliked dogs.

CHAPTER SEVEN

Spunky Amoun in Trouble

In retrospect, I had a colorful childhood that had both happiness and sadness. Being a Gypsy certainly made things more interesting. The mount near the cemetery at the Lions' Gate holds many childhood memories. I loved sitting near the gate in the green spring landscape looking to the other side toward the Mount of Olives and the Church of Gethsemane. All the little girls of the community met there and played. Sometimes we had a kilo of bananas. We were not there just because of the bananas, but for the view. Our parents were afraid for us to be near the cemetery for fear that someone might harm us. We went anyway. It was especially beautiful in the spring with masses of yellow flowers and red poppies.

As kids, we could get in trouble even at celebrations. We liked to dance at weddings. We would jump in between the partners who were dancing, and they would push us away. The tradition at a Gypsy wedding is for the old people to dance together with even men and women dancing together. The family of the bride will dance together, then the family of the groom will have a dance. I broke the tradition and joined with anyone who was dancing.

Helge, a Swedish tourist who Amoun helped and who became a family friend.

When we saw pilgrims from all over the world coming to the Church of Gethsemane, we moved quickly to be present beside them to sell pictures of Jerusalem so we could get candy and money. People who sold daily near the church ran after us. Some of them hated us, but we had good times with the tourists. They gave us love and attention. We were heroes for many people over there because we would warn tourists if someone was trying to steal from them, or we would help them in other ways.

Once when I was about eight years old, a big bus brought people from a cruise ship to visit Gethsemane. Someone saw me and gave me a beautiful huge piece of fruit. Others saw and started doing the same. As they came down the stairs from the bus, they gave me their lunch bags. I had all this food. But there was a powerful Gypsy woman who took things that were not hers. The mentality of that family is when good things happen, it means money for them. I hid the food and looked to see if she was watching. There she was at the gate. I knew she would take it away. I thought, "Amoun, what can you do?" I took the bags up the hill with the power God gave me and crawled through a very small window in the Old City wall. My father said, "If God is with you, you don't need people."

When I was just ten years old, I used to have fun with a small group of Gypsy girls. Our usual play spot where we used to run up and down, sit, and talk to each other was just outside the Lions' Gate. One Sunday, our holiday, we saw many men walk together holding something tightly which they put into the ground. After they left, we went over to investigate and uncovered a beautiful sleeping baby. We took the baby and played with it all day. We even brought it home and showed it to my neighbor, who happened to be visiting. She fainted and nearly had a heart attack. The baby was dead. We took the baby back to its resting place. That night my father gave me a nice gift—a spanking and a rule that I could not go out of the house for two days. I asked my grandmother to talk to him. He only relented a little. To this day, that neighbor reminds me how bad I was.

When I was a child, there was a period of two years that I dropped out of school. I dropped out of school after fifth grade. Two years later when I returned to school, I started back in sixth grade. My parents knew that I stopped going to school. I was scared and crying all the time, so my father said it was my decision. My grandmother knew my fear also, and let me decide. When I dropped out, I hung out in the neighborhood around the Lion's Gate. Sometimes the adult Gypsies would send me on an errand for them. The Gypsy woman who controlled the neighborhood would send me to buy falafel or something else so that her children would be the ones who would get to talk to the tourists. We were always being pushed from place to place. There were seasons that tourists were around. The tourists saw us hanging around and would give us money to take our pictures. This gave me the idea of how to make money by posing for their cameras. Their kindness and generosity was too high. When we were twelve or thirteen, the generosity began to look more like begging to me. At that time, I really felt like I wanted something different. I asked myself, "What are they thinking about me?"

During this time, I got into many accidents. I was more afraid of punishment from my father than anything else. One time a group of Gypsy girls and I were taken to the police station because they said running after the tourists was forbidden.

These were the Arab police who cooperated with vendors who sold postcards in the street. I think they did this to scare us. Those sellers wanted us out of the streets so they would get the business. I was scared to death of what my father would do to me.

Three of the Gypsy girls were not afraid at all. They came to me and said, "Let's change our names and the names of our parents." One of the girls gave the name of our neighbor so they could not find her. I had to smile because this neighbor was a simple man who didn't have children. The police knew this and could see that we were playing with them.

In the end, they became sick of us and our games. They said, "Go home, and we don't want to see you back here." We weren't really bad, and they weren't really harsh with us. They just wanted to keep us off the streets and away from the tourists.

I went home and tried to hide the story, but I couldn't keep it from my grandmother. She saw how scared I was and gave me a hug. She said that the truth will always come alive. She tried to help me see that I didn't have to worry about telling the truth even when I was scared.

Another time there was a fight inside the Lions' Gate between two men right in front of St. Anne's church. One of them held a glass and tried to hit the other man. I was standing too close, was hit by the glass, and began to bleed.

I should have been worried about my face, but I was more worried about what my father would say. Some people who saw me took me to the nearby clinic. The doctor began to sew stitches near my eye. I couldn't even feel the pain because I was worrying that my dad would think I had again put my nose into more trouble.

My grandmother, as usual, understood my situation and explained it to my dad. The day ended with a good soup that my grandmother made for my dad, my family, and me. She thought I needed a lot of food because I had lost so much blood. My brother, Belial said, "I hope you will have an accident like this more often so that we can have a good meal."

Sometimes my own choices got me into trouble. My grandmother made very good food with grape leaves. She made one layer of zucchini, a layer of meat, and then a layer of grape leaves. This *warak dewwali* was a specialty of hers.

One day, a woman in the community who was always taking things that did not belong to her organized a trip to the Dead Sea for many kids. She told me to go home and bring some food for the trip. I wanted to go on the trip, but I didn't have any money or food for the trip. I went to the kitchen, saw the pan of warak dewwali, and took the entire pan to the woman.

I knew trouble was coming, but I wanted to go so bad. I knew it was wrong. I couldn't really enjoy the trip because of my worry inside. I felt like a white angel was talking to me the whole trip telling me that what I did was wrong.

This was the meal for my entire family. When my grandmother discovered the missing food, she began to shout, "Where's the pan!" She continued to shout until I returned from the trip with the empty pan.

She yelled, "Yasser, she took the entire meal!" I got in so much trouble. My grandmother asked the woman why she took the entire pan from a child. The woman just blamed it on me, and that night I got a "nice" spanking that I will not forget.

I remember we used to go to the Lions' Gate where a man sold a delicious juice called carob juice. The man was named Halawani, which means sweet. So the sweet man sold a sweet drink. It would take half of the money we earned in a day to buy the juice. We also thought we could forget the family and spend the other half of our money on the falafel and humus. We loved the warm pita bread and falafel and spent everything we earned to share this meal and juice.

The postcards we sold cost only $1. We could not say another number even if we wanted to because we didn't speak English very well. Sometimes the tourists would give us four dollars or five dollars. My father and grandmother expected me to bring that money home, but I spent the money on my stomach instead of thinking of my family.

When we went home, we told our families, "We didn't make anything today."

My grandmother said, "I think you were playing all day." The second day we had to make up for what we spent. We had to start thinking about our families. We began to say, "one for you, and ten for others." This is an expression meaning you should have more concern for others than for yourself.

Twice a year we had holidays. The holidays were a period of dreams, and we got new clothes. The dreams allowed us to do small things we loved to do. Our parents, including my father, allowed us to go to the Jerusalem Cinema in Al-Zahra Street. Usually, Gypsy men worked in the cinema with ticketing and selling sandwiches.

Our father gave us a little money to buy a sandwich and a ticket. They were movies from India that were safe for children to watch and related to our culture. We enjoyed going with a group of boys and girls. We bought the cheap tickets for the lower class seats, but we knew there were many Gypsy men working in the cinema, and they would put us in the middle class. We felt like we were in high station!

Sometimes we would watch the movie three times because it was the only place we were allowed to go on the holidays. We would enjoy it so much. Even on the way home, the group of girls discussed the beautiful ending of the movie with each other.

By the time I was twelve years old, I stopped being interested in children's games. I looked mature like I was sixteen. Even men began to notice me. On Fridays and Sundays, we liked to go down to the Lions' Gate and Gethsemane. Instead of having fun as I did two years earlier, I sold postcards to earn money. My friends and I also helped tourists do things so we could earn some pocket money for the week. I would offer to help anyone and everyone in order to save a few dollars for school. This contradicted the notion that Gypsies only make money to spend it the next day.

Once a lady accidentally put her expensive ring in my hand with the money for the postcards. The ring must have been loose and come off. I hurried to give it back to her. The money for the ring would have been a lot, but I had three things I had to think about. I knew when I returned to my family, they would ask, "Where did you get this?" They did not approve of anything that was not received honestly. Second, the ring did not belong to me. Finally, our family focus was on survival, not on taking things for riches that did not belong to us

We were not welcomed anywhere we went in the local community, but the tourists were different. They seemed to like us and treated us kindly. Helping the many tourists who visited the Old City regularly gave us the advantage of meeting different people from all around the world. They gave us sweets, money, and even clothes because we Gypsies are fun, happy people. It made my life happier to meet people from all over the world.

Sometimes helping tourists caused us problems. One time I heard a woman scream. Without thinking, I ran to help her even though I did not speak English well. She was Swedish and did not speak English either. We talked with hand signals. I saw that she had been attacked, and someone had stolen her money. She could tell from my face that I was trying to help her. I told her that my name was Amoun and brought her to my home. I gave her some treatment for her wounds and a cup of tea. After that, I brought her to the nearest police station. Even with all her tears and pain, she was thankful and glad to see that there was also good in this country.

I went home and told the story to my friends. That afternoon, just as my father was returning home from work, the police knocked on my door asking for me. I will never forget the look on my father's face—the face of "What did you do now, Amoun?"

The police said they wanted to take me back to the station to question me. I started to cry. I told my father that I did not do anything wrong and asked him to believe me. It was a scary situation. I went back to the station with them.

As it turned out, the police did not understand what the woman was telling them because she spoke only Swedish. When she gave them my name, they thought I was behind what happened to her instead of someone who had helped her. It was not until they brought a man to talk to her in Swedish and translate that everything got sorted out.

In the end, the police became red in the face, and I got a kiss from this woman. We stayed in touch for many years. She wrote postcards to me and sent me small gifts from Sweden. After that experience, I have always told myself I would be there for people who need me even if it costs me or causes me trouble.

In the area near Gethsemane, there was an Arab man that the Gypsy girls feared. He was a large man and all of the children, especially us girls, were ordered to avoid him. When he saw us, he would hit us and take all the money we had collected that day. One day after I had a long day of working hard, he tried to catch me and take my money. I ran from him. Just as he was about to catch and hit me, I pushed him so hard that he fell and broke three of his teeth. I could hardly believe I had the power in me to do that.

I was both happy and worried. On the one hand, I took on a large man that everyone was scared of and earned the right to sell in that area without his threat. On the other hand, I knew it would cause trouble for my family, and they already had problems enough of their own. Since I hit a man, everyone was afraid. I didn't believe it myself. He had already caused harm in our neighborhood. I was especially afraid to see my father's face. He gave me a look that frightened me, and that I will never forget.

I've never been afraid like that before, but in the eyes of the Gypsy girls I was a hero! I had done something no one had dared to do before. The man was from an influential family and could cause problems for my Gypsy family. This family could also ask for money for damages I caused.

I did not feel like a hero. In truth, inside me I felt like a fool and cried about what I had done. At the same time, I knew that if I had not stopped this bully, it would have been me with the broken teeth. He would continue to do bad things to me and nobody would stop him. I was even more powerless as a Gypsy girl. Since my family was Gypsy, there was nothing they could do either. In the end, his family was ashamed and did not say anything about a little girl hitting a grown man.

After that day, I became a leader for the girls. I looked after them, and they listened to me. We cared about each other. Because of this, we were able to establish our place in that area to sell postcards and meet tourists. We still had our problems, and people often treated us badly. We never really had any peace. We had to think carefully about everything we did for fear of the people around us. We didn't have any way around our problems. They grew every day as we grew up. After this event, I realized that people will never leave you in peace. I learned that one must think before one acts because there is no way to escape problems.

Beside playing and teasing people when I was a child, I had some talent to create things. I remember many times making something from nothing. I would collect the garbage and old furniture that people threw away and try to clean it up to be used.

I really liked working with plants. Plants for me are something very important and close to my soul. When I feel sadness, a little bit depressed, or nervous, I like to plant something. I like to replace that hurt or anger with something bright and happy. It pleases me to go to gardens where I can see different plants and flowers. This is a hobby and is joyful for me. I used to do some gardening in other people's yards.

I also like to paint, even though I don't have the skill for it. Sometimes people tell me I'm really a Gypsy because I mix up many bright colors in my pictures. I really like the bright colors together.

There are other skills I like but do not have, such as sewing and crocheting. I have no hand or skill for it, but I put my hopes and wishes with the women in my community who do have that skill. The sewing that I wished to see in myself is now something that I help other women to do through the work of the Domari Community Center.

CHAPTER EIGHT

Gypsy Marriage Customs

In our community, a Gypsy girl is typically married off by the time she is fifteen or sixteen years old. She and the boy she is marrying usually have little or no education. This causes dependency on his immediate family for food and living expenses. I think some of these young girls can only see the joy of the wedding day and the gifts and gold they receive. Sometimes the marriage ends with divorce because they were not mature, and it was difficult for them to get used to the new life.

After a year of marriage, a bride is expected to have her first child. If not, the family will talk about her and send her to a fertility doctor. If that fails, her husband will divorce her, and she will return to her family, only to be remarried to another man. According to tradition, the best life for a woman is to be with a husband.

An example of the importance of having children comes from my own family. My grandfather, Shaker Ibrahim married a woman named Zarifeh who was about seventeen. She was a specialist in spices and natural medicine. She discovered that she could not have children. This was dishonorable. She said a man without kids was like tree without leaves and offered to help him find a second wife. This second wife, Amina, was my father's mother. We considered them both to be our grandmothers. Some of us were closer to one and some to the other. I was named for the second grandmother, Amina, and my sister Zarifeh was named for the first grandmother. My sister Chadra was also named after a woman on my father's side.

My name is complicated. It is a double name because my mother and father called me by the name they preferred. Amouneh is an ancient, Egyptian name. Since my mother was Egyptian, she liked this popular name and called me Amoun. My father preferred the name Amina because it was his mother's name. So, I answered to both Amoun and Amina.

I remember that my grandmothers loved each other although they often disagreed—like Tom and Jerry. When my grandfather died, they continued to live together as sisters.

When it came to marriage, our father gave us a lot of freedom from the old practices. According to the custom, it is important that Gypsies do not marry outside the community. If a girl marries outside the community, she will be excommunicated. Girls from the Old City may marry outside the community, but only to Gypsies from Jordan. The prospects for marrying someone from Jordan are no different than marrying someone from the Old City. Like those in Jerusalem, Jordanian Gypsies have no education and marry young. The only thing a Gypsy girl can do is make her house look nice and bring up as many children as she can even if her husband does not work. What kind of life is this?

Gypsy girls are told the story of the man who fell in love with a Gypsy girl and asked for her hand in marriage numerous times. Her family refused this man every time even though the girl was in love with him, too. The lovers had no choice but to run away and elope. Her family was very sad and disrespectful to them. They no longer welcomed them. No one has forgotten this story, especially us Gypsy girls. The story gives little hope for us Gypsy girls to live a life of freedom or to choose the man we would like to love and marry.

My father allowed us to say no to any man who came to ask our hands in marriage. All he wanted was the best for his daughters as well as for his sons. He allowed two of my brothers to marry girls from other communities, who never had any contact with Gypsies before. My father's open-mindedness was considered by the rest of the community to be breaking the rules, which caused many problems for him. The community people acted as if my father's nose was high, as if he thought he was better than them, but he didn't. They told him, "You should say yes if someone comes for your daughter." Such radical behavior as his was unheard of. To this day, my sisters and I remain unwed. I have simply not found the right person, and I do not feel sorry one bit. Thanks to my father, I have managed to reach the level where I am in life and am able to write my story.

It is also a tradition for Gypsies to have tattoos—for medicine like acupuncture or for beauty. For either a man or woman, a single dot tattoo on the face is a sign that you are a Gypsy. Usually, they start getting them when they are about seventeen. My father got a large one when he was a young man, but he regretted it later.

I make up my mind for myself, like my father. I only got one tattoo when I was very young. I wiped it off, leaving only a faint mark. I did not get them because they were painful and because I thought they were ugly. Some of my friends said I was a loser, but I am a character who does what I like. Why should I do something because somebody else does it?

CHAPTER NINE

Two Grandmothers

My grandmother Amina was special to me. She was a lot like my mom and took care of me so well. I called her "Dadi" in the Dom language. She had a great heart. Because of my mother's death, I spent more time with her than with my mom.

My grandmother Zarifeh had amazing energy for people all around her, many she hardly knew. In her eyes, they were all the same—human. She never closed her door to people, which caused a problem with her husband. He told her, "You act like a wife for everyone, not just for me." If there was a wedding, she was the first to cook for and fix the bride, to sing a song for her. She was there to draw happiness on people's faces.

My grandmother Amina used to have some simple financial assistance from the government, but she used this money to help us live. She would say, "Make your wish, and I will try to make it happen." She bought us *shawarma* that we always dreamed of eating. This is meat cooked on a spit for as long as a day. Shavings are cut off for eating. She never kept her little money for herself, which was her right. We would have liked to go to a restaurant, but

(From left to right) Amoun's sister Chadra (child), Grandmother Zarifeh, Hyatt, Grandmother Amina, Amoun's mother Miriam, amd Fouseh (Miriam's sister).

there was no money for that. Instead, when my grandmother got money, she would buy the *shawarma* and chicken from a rotisserie for a treat and bring it home while it was still warm. We would wait at the Lions' Gate to help her up the many steps with her big bags.

If we didn't have guests, we usually didn't eat meat. We had bread called *shrek*, baked over the fire by my grandmother in a twenty-inch circle. The bread was paper thin, even thinner than a wrap. If she was in a good mood, she spread it with olive oil and sugar or olive oil and special spices. We ate bread with grapes, bread with watermelon, and bread with goat cheese. We ate rice, beans, lentils, and many fresh vegetables. When we had meat we usually had chicken, but sometimes my father would buy turkey instead. I said it before—I didn't like turkey.

During the war, for a long time the United Nations gave people flour and some food at the Lions' Gate. Food coupons were issued to refugees. My grandmother had a card to be punched when she received food with the name and number of children in the household. She lost hers so she didn't have a card to receive the flour. She used her mind and said people need little bags to hold all this food. So she made handbags from cloth to give them in exchange for some of the flour. She was thinking a little from here and a little from there will get a large amount of flour into the house.

I never had a doll like any other kids. I had one my grandmother Zarifeh made for me. It was the most beautiful one. She had beads for eyes, hair from leftover thread in all sorts of crazy colors. My grandmother made her all kinds of dresses. I talked to the doll and made her my friend. Sometimes I called the doll names I found in cartoons or children's stories, like Snederlaa. I loved my mom, so sometimes I called her by my mom's name, Laila. Other times, I would call her by a friend's name so I could feel like I was still talking to the friend. She was a simple doll, and I dressed her like a child. I loved her, and she was always with me.

Both of my grandmothers were beautiful storytellers. They told stories from experiences in life and from their imaginations. They told stories of the lives of the Dom who lived adventures. They traveled from place to place and lived difficult lives based on respect. Even when there was a period of war or fear, they lived with their chances but always looked for hope and a new day.

I loved to hear the stories of the period in the Six Days War. My grandmother Zarifeh was the Superman. She fought not with weapons, but with love in order to survive with her family who needed her in that time.

Both of them told other very beautiful stories. Zarifeh told the story of the hyena named Amora who looked human and told you things you wanted to hear. The hyena came to the ones she wanted to be close to, bringing gold, and granting wishes. The story called attention to being excluded from family and the large responsibility of parents. Her stories distracted us from our problems. The fantasies make me smile now as I remember the stories she told about Daba Daba, who stole kids and took them far away. If you weren't good, she would take you away from your parents. The stories might seem scary, but we begged her to tell them over and over.

In school, I had problems with a teacher. She always hit me on the hand with a piece of wood. One day I went back to the house with my hands blue and in pain. My grandmother Amina said, "This is enough and must be stopped."

She went to the teacher and said, "If you don't stop hitting my grand-daughter, I will give you a lesson that you will never forget all your life."

I was so happy inside, but I was also afraid of what would happen next. Without fear, my grandmother protected me. She taught me to bear responsibility for my sisters and myself and to support my father. She also gave a lesson to this teacher on humanity and non-discrimination toward the Dom clan.

Many years later, I was asked to speak to a large group. That teacher was in the audience, but she did not recognize me. As a member of the community, she tried to speak with me afterwards about the children dropping out of the school. At that moment, I could not open my mouth to talk with her. I could not forget how she treated me in her class. I had to ignore her as if she was not there because of the painful memories that she brought to my mind.

My grandmother Zarifeh had a place in the life of the Dom and worked to help their lives. She was a mother and father all the time and for all the people. She was a great woman, but simple at the same time. She worked hard in a life that was not easy. The community considered her as its nurse even though she was not trained. She treated adults and children in the Dom clan without charge. She rarely said no to anyone. She was one of the best practitioners of alternative medicine and invented new remedies. She always looked for good "weeds" that were beneficial to the human body.

Sometimes Zarifeh served as a midwife. She mixed olive oil soap shavings and egg white until it was the consistency of glue. She spread it on paper and plastered it on the forehead for migraines. Her patients said the migraines went away.

People brought her soap to use for their cures, and she took the shavings she needed. Maybe they brought olive oil for a child's medicine. She used a few drops. Whatever was left of the soap or olive oil was her payment to keep. She put whatever people brought her in bags all over the house. We would go in her room looking, and she would say, "Out! Out!"

When she left the house, we went looking to see what we could find in her room. She would come back and say to my father, "Yasser, they're stealing my stuff."

He would say to us, "Go out!"

Even with the little we had, there was hospitality. Once when I was young, I found a very tall woman at the Lions' Gate. I had never seen anyone so tall, and I brought her home for the family to see. My grandmother Zarifeh gave her tea, and she gave us some money.

Several days later, she came back at night wearing solid white. Someone had tried to rob her. She came running into our house without knocking and rushed into my grandmother's room. My grandmother screamed, "Yasser!" She thought a ghost had come.

My father came running. With our little English and hand language, we found out what had happened. My father said, "She can sleep here. Amoun, make a place."

The mattress was too short, and the blanket even shorter. Ten people slept in the room that night. The woman kept in touch for many years.

I miss a memory of my grandmother Zarifeh at home. Every morning her two sisters came visiting like they had been dreaming of each other. My grandmother made tea for the others. They sat on the ground close to each other near the wall of Jerusalem where we lived. They talked and admired the beautiful view like a queen and her assistants. They told each other how their week had been and took advice from my grandmother, even though she was the middle sister. They sat until noontime and then made lunch together on the fire. They pushed me to go play with kids and come back when the food was ready, but I preferred to be with them and listen to their stories. A strong feeling grew inside me that I see myself more with the old people who sit and talk than with people my own age. Later, they would invite other old ladies from the community to come join them. Sometimes, I wish I could go back to these memories.

My grandmothers had a beautiful fig tree. They gave abnormal care to this tree, treating it like one of their kids. They cleaned and talked to it and sat under it most days. When it started to grow, they painted it with olive oil to make it shine and to strengthen the tree to make it bear even more fruit. When my grandmother Amina died, the tree disappeared just like there had never been one there in the first place. My family said they knew that animals like a horse or dog get sick and die if they lose their boss, but to see a tree get sad is impossible! But my grandmothers were impossible women, always giving—even to plants. I believe that flowers or trees can listen to you and can give to you if you give to them. I am not surprised.

I will never forget my father when his mother Amina died in the hospital. He knelt on the ground, touching her feet, crying hard like I didn't see him cry even for my mother when she died. We all loved this great mother and lovely one!

My grandmother Zarifeh was a simple human being who liked to work. She did not like a lazy man. I learned a lot from her. She was a fighter in a good way. We had a poor background, but we never felt it because she could create something from nothing. We brought wood for her fire, and she made the tastiest bread for us and to share with the neighbors. She was the great queen for both Gypsies and non-Gypsies. She had nothing, but she was the richest woman of her time because of her great hospitality and sharing. Perhaps I am what I am because of what I learned from my grandmother's presence in my life.

CHAPTER TEN

My Father, Managing Alone

After my grandmother's death, my father had to care for his children alone. Finally, he and my oldest sister Amar, who was fifteen, decided that she would stop going to school and help in the house. Both of my grandmothers taught Amar how to cook and care for the family and the house. She became like a mother to the rest of the children, including my brothers Ali, Shaker, Mohamed, Rajab, and Bilal. She gave her life for her family. Even now, she is not married and continues to care for us.

My father worked very hard in a part time job as a guard at the Ministry of the Interior. He would come home at noon to be with us. Rajab was a baby then, and my father liked to hold him all the time. At work, my father was the right hand of Mrs. Sabeh, the head of the ministry. They made ID cards, birth certificates, travel permits, and other documents. Sometimes I took requests from my teachers in high school because they knew he could help them get their papers quickly.

My father could not read or write. When he got a letter from the government, he would send one of us to the neighbor to find out what it said. He was embarrassed and wanted better things for his children. Even though he could not read or write Arabic, my father had talents with languages. He learned some Hebrew at work and picked up some English from tourists who visited our home.

For many years, we did not have water inside our home. We had to buy water from our neighbor and put it in a large tank that was near the kitchen. My father got permission to put water pipes and sewage service in our house when I was a teenager.

When we were kids, some of us had a bath inside in a round metal tub. My oldest sister Amar made us take a bath four times a week while most Gypsies bathed once a week. I thought she was punishing us. She washed us with homemade olive oil soap that burned our eyes if it ran down. Of course, it always burned our eyes because she had to wash our long hair and pour the water over us three or four times. I never had real shampoo until I was fourteen or fifteen years old.

My father was not rich, but he tried to give us a good life. He always said, "He who has no past will never have a future." He pushed us to be proud and remember the nice and good times we had when we were children.

I am thankful that I had such a good-natured and kind father, and for Amar, a selfless sister who completely gave her life to us, to the point that even now she remains unwed. Thanks to these two beacons of light, the rest of us had a life of opportunity found by very few in our community. When we grew up, we tried to help as soon as we could.

CHAPTER ELEVEN

My Family

Every Gypsy family likes to have many children. I come from a family of nine children—five brothers and four sisters. My father was proud of his family. All of my brothers and sisters have faced discrimination because we are Gypsies. We all encourage one another not to fight back when people say things against us. I'd love to share about my dear brothers and sisters, their lives, and their roles in the family.

My oldest brother Shaker passed away on November 28, 2012. He was the big brother, a very giving person who looked after everyone in the family. His death left a big space in the family. He married Fatima, a very good cook. They raised five good kids.

Heubia is sixteen. She hopes to finish high school and go to university. Sometimes she wants to be a graphic designer. Other times she wants to be a teacher.

Fourteeen-year-old Yasser hasn't decided what he wants to be, but we will be glad if he finishes high school. He likes technical things and loves to fix things. A good present for him is a box of tools.

Sadeen is eight. I think she has a good future if she continues to do what she does right now. She is second in her class. She will keep asking questions until she gets it right. She wants 100 on her paper, not 99. We are hoping for a medical profession since she is very serious for her age.

Dania is four and in kindergarten. She is a difficult child and is very strong. She has a big mouth and will talk back to you. When she wants something, she needs to have it, but she is great looking with a great smile.

Abdullah is three and in kindergarten. He is easy-going, loves cars, and likes to play all the time.

Amar, the oldest sister and the second child after Shaker, took over after my mom died. She cared for all of us with the help of my grandmother. She learned cooking from my grandmother. She loves to give and feed people. She did not finish school but gave her life for her family becoming both sister and mother for all. She makes the best tea in the world.

Chadra, the funny smile sister, is very kind and never says no to anyone. She loves to clean and keep things in order. She left school at an early age because she loves laughter and fun. She likes to wake up every day at 6:30 and starts her day by cleaning the house.

She studied hairdressing. She can imitate anybody. Trying to please sometimes gets her in trouble. A man asked her for help with his ATM card. She didn't know anything about it, but she always wants to help out. She told him to put it in a slot, push this button and that button, and then the machine ate his card.

Zarifeh, the third sister and my good example in life, taught me that life doesn't always come to you, you have to go to it. She worked hard for the future when she was very young. She is the first trained nurse in the community. Often Zarifeh must work the hours at the hospital that the other nurses do not want. Even though she has much experience, she has been passed over for higher positions all because she is a Gypsy. She watched my mother go into the hospital and loved nursing from an early age. She never gives up when she wants something. She took the Jewish nursing exam many times because she was determined to pass. Now she is both a nurse and works in hospice care. She was my father's nurse more than the ones in the hospital.

Zarifeh works hard and helps the family financially. She gives a lot and receives very little. She tries to save money for improvements in the family because she is trying to bring stability to the family. I buy something for her when I buy for myself because I know she doesn't buy for herself. I have to push her sometimes to do things for enjoyment. She is like a supporting wall for the family. It's so good to have such a sister.

Amoun Sleem (me, in the middle) is a simple Gypsy woman looking for hope and wishing for change. She has deep love for her brothers and sisters. She looks at the world with many eyes, some full of pain, and still hopes to change the future.

Mohammed, the second brother, married Keytam. My brother is a simple man, full of kindness, who didn't finish school. He works hard and does as much as he can to please others. He and his wife try to help their three girls and two boys finish school and get a good education. Keytam works with the kids every day to help them do their homework and encourages them to be good in school.

Laila is sixteen years old and in high school. She likes to design apparel and always draws nice clothes. I do hope she reaches her dream.

Nine-year old Doha doesn't always study. She just likes to draw and make colors everywhere.

Once she got in trouble at school. The teacher asked, "Where is the wall of Jerusalem?"

Doha answered, "In my home."

The teacher was not happy. She thought she had a lying student. She didn't know that a person could climb right over the wall from the house. Doha's dark eyes turned red because she was so afraid of the teacher's anger.

Yumna is seven. She has good handwriting and loves to draw. She's very sure of herself. She has a mind of her own and a vision. She dreams to one day be a doctor. I believe she will if she keeps her same level of schoolwork.

Youssef, in kindergarten and four years old, has the most beautiful smile. He always smiles and is crazy with cars. I hope that his future has a company with cars that he always dreams about.

Omar is two years old. He is an easy-going child and likes to always be with me. I enjoy seeing him around.

Ali is married to Bahirah. Ali is my closest brother. We have good talks when he is around doing things. He has been involved in helping with the work at the Domari Center with some of the catering courses.

About 2002, Ali was working in construction on a big machine, a digger. He was terribly injured when the electronic system on the machine failed. He was in intensive care for two weeks and almost died. In those moments, we brought his one-year-old daughter to the hospital so he could feel someone near that he should fight to live for, even though he was unconscious. That was his lovely daughter Amar.

I will never forget my father's tears one day when we were visiting the hospital as we did daily. The doctor said, "Your son has woken up." My father cried like a child, and he was thankful to God. Ali went through several surgeries at that time, but this guy was fighting for his life, his daughter, and his family.

Even now, I call him the fighter because he doesn't have a 100 percent body. He doesn't give up. Now, he is a taxi driver with a big heart. I am proud of his kindness with his family and his open hand with others. I see him as a great father. His care for his daughters is unique for a Gypsy man. Waking up and taking them to school every day is different from other Gypsy men. His wife is a good cook and loves to feed other people. They have three girls and one boy.

Amar is thirteen years old and very good in high school. She says when she is sure of her dreams, she will tell them all to us.

Batual is a nine-year-old dreamer who has her own way. She has a beautiful face for sure. She likes to help and clean. If she does something bad, she says, "I didn't do it." She is lovable and does well in school.

Sarah is a sweet five-year-old who likes to draw. She is close friends with Yumna, and they share secrets which no one can know.

Adam, a good-looking two-year-old, likes to touch everything. He is not easy at all and drives his mother and father crazy.

Belal is married to Melanie, and they have a two-year-old daughter. They call her Sherri, but her name in Arabic is Rasha. Belal has his own way of thinking and made choices different from the other brothers who followed my dad's example in building their families.

Rasha is quiet, almost two, and looks Indian because her mother is from Sri Lanka. In the beginning, she didn't like Gypsy food.

Rajab, the last brother, married Roba. They have a son and daughter. Rajab is a funny person who knows everyone. He loves food and eats many sweets. That's why he has the biggest stomach among my brothers, but that is also his choice. They have a son and a daughter.

Retaj will soon be in kindergarten. In the beginning, she is shy, but after she gets used to you, she will cling and cry when you leave. She has beautiful hair and eyes and is a dreamer.

Ismael is just a baby. We will see.

I have really nice brothers. Two of them are married to girls not from the Gypsy community. These people like us and think other people have the wrong idea about Gypsies. They were glad to give their girls to my brothers. They live happily together, but the Gypsy people don't like it. They ask, "Why didn't they take a wife from the community?" We don't mind. We are happy with their choice.

CHAPTER TWELVE

Break with Tradition or Not?

Other Gypsy men have not been so fortunate. One of the most lovely kind men in our community fell in love with a non-Gypsy woman. Her family didn't know he was Gypsy, and he thought it best not to tell them. The family approved of the marriage. He loved the daughter, and she loved him. Everything seemed fine, and he was as happy as he had ever been in his life. Two days before the wedding, someone told the family that the man their daughter was about to marry was a Gypsy. On the day the wedding was to take place, the family told him, "We have no daughter to give in marriage." They returned the gold and other things he had given for the wedding. Today he has a good job and a nice life. At fifty-two, he has never married, but he says, "Even though it has caused me pain, I am still proud to be a Gypsy."

The Gypsy lifestyle is different and unique in other ways. Typically, Gypsies do not like to get mixed up with other communities. They have often given up hope of making a better life for their children and never seek to open doors or to change. Like other communities in the Middle East, you belong to your family until you marry or you die.

Unfortunately, begging has been taught and passed down from generation to generation. Because of poverty, poor job situations, and a welfare system that seems to encourage dependence, the easiest way to make money seems to be begging. Memories of begging as a child on the street haunt the mind of an adult like a black mark. Begging has come to be the picture associated in people's minds when they hear the word "Gypsy." It is very unfair for the children because there is no future in this never-ending cycle as these children grow up to be like their fathers.

The tourists were kind to us, but the people from the neighborhood called us "the begging people," and some still do. They have not forgotten when our people had to beg in the past. This leads to the purpose of having a community center—to create awareness among the Gypsies that they can make their dreams come true. We want to show that the past is past, and the future is still the future. Even though this culture has gone through difficult periods that caused our people to beg, the future can be new.

Some people also think of Gypsies as wasteful people. One example that supports this idea is the way Gypsies welcome their guests. Our hospitality comes in the form of feeding our guests three days in our home. We end up cooking many different kinds of food as well as offering elaborate gifts, which adds up to major expense. We feel we must never let our guests know that we cannot afford this.

Day-by-day living is also reflected in Gypsies not owning their own homes. It is not our mentality to pay for or buy a home or purchase a plot of land. For Gypsies living in the Old City, it was easier to buy land before the creation of Israel (1948). Instead, Gypsies marry off their children at a young age to have even more children because they believe multiplying will bring them more power.

Instead of saving money to buy a house or set up a business, Gypsies will typically spend all of their money on a wedding. It is traditional for the groom's family to pay the father of the bride a lot of gold. Much money is spent on the meal before the wedding, which must have enough food and sweets to feed all the wedding guests. The couple getting married are practically children themselves. The groom has no money to call his own and must rely on his family for support.

Usually, Gypsies do not have any education. Most children grow up on the streets. This is what their families choose as the best school for them. The rationalization is that children will go to work on the streets early. Even if they do bad things, they are only children. I can count on one hand the number of Gypsy people I know who have actually finished school.

I grew up in this culture, but with this big fire inside me because I knew there was no future in this way of life. Fortunately, my father was different from other Gypsies and understood the importance of education. I was allowed to go to the Arabic school in the Old City. Even with a supportive father, it was not easy. We had no electricity at home. I, as well as my brothers and sisters, did our homework at night by candlelight.

My father also broke with tradition in other ways. It was uncommon for a Gypsy girl to make deals with businessmen. Even older women are meant to be in the house, not in public business with men. When we were able to make improvements to our home, my father gave me permission and sent me out to negotiate for the cement and the construction plans. I think he was preparing me for my later life.

CHAPTER THIRTEEN

Dealing with Discrimination

Even though I was a good child, I could not escape the discrimination against me for being a Gypsy. I would always be considered a rotten child from a rotten community, who should have no rights to access education. We were discriminated against at school by teachers and classmates. To this day, I will never forget the disgust on the face of this one teacher, the head of the school. When she looked at me and other Gypsy girls, we must have looked like animals in her eyes. If she could have had her way, she would have banned all Gypsies from attending school. Luckily, she did not have this power.

It did not prevent her from scarring me for life. One day when I was in fifth grade, she said to me, "You are like a flea in this world, and you must be annihilated."

After that, my world turned upside down. She hurt my feelings in a big way. I started to ask myself, "Why do people hate each other this way? What did I do for this woman to treat me so badly?" I changed. I did not want to go to school to study. I was afraid of this teacher. My marks at school

Staff of the Dutch Guest House where Amoun and Khadra worked. Kaise is on the left and Coby is the 4th person from the left.

changed, too. I failed two years in school. I had no power to study. I spent many a night crying and stewing on what she said to me. I lost two years of study because of that teacher.

After a long time of crying and thinking, I remembered my mother and what she said to me. "Always, I want you to be a good girl and a nice girl." I thought a lot about my mother, and I went back to a normal life. I said to myself that if I finished primary school, I would move to high school and my problems would stop.

I was wrong. The same thing happened in high school. I think it was written on our faces, "We are Gypsies. Watch out!" The only difference this time was that I made a nice set of Arab friends, and together with keeping a smile on my face, I managed to get through each day. I was determined to get a good education, and I was sure God would help me achieve my goals. Throughout high school, it was a struggle for me and my family in our one room to find a good time to study. I could only study at night while everyone else wanted to sleep. We made it work because we knew education was important.

By the time I entered high school, as I was studying and working, I found solid work as an extra pair of hands alongside my sister Chadra, at a nice Dutch guesthouse on the Mount of Olives. Chadra was already working there three days a week. When she heard that the owners were looking for another girl to help out, she thought of me because of my English. My sisters Zarifeh and Chadra had very mediocre English. They practiced, "Welcome, to drink tea?" to people passing by, but I knew that English was important to my future. From the very first day I started working there, I liked it.

The one good thing I learned from the street was my English from the tourists. I came from a normal school in the Old City where they don't teach English until the 6th grade class. My English was five-star compared to the other kids, but my teachers didn't know my background with the language. It had come from running after tourists and learning to talk to them using hand signals. It made me feel like I was in private school. The teachers were angry with me. They asked, "Why are your marks much better in English than in Arabic? Are your parents English?"

I answered, "No, Dom people." That drove them crazy, but it was an honest answer given from an honest heart.

My father had to come in to the high school for a conference. The teacher said, "Amoun is a good student, but she has a big mouth and talks too much."

My father said to me, "You can't close your mouth?"

I said, "I'll try."

I knew this job at the Dutch house was the start of a different life and would lead to better opportunities for me. Some girls in my community thought that I would never make it, that I would end up having to find a man to marry. They thought I was like a lion, someone who wanted to have everything. What they did not know is that I was not a lion. I was simply striving for things they never tried to have.

I wanted to show them they were wrong. I wanted to make changes and make my dreams come true. My dream was to go to college. I knew I would have to work hard and wait because my dreams were not yet attainable due to financial circumstances, loyalty to the family, and the need to work and bring income to the family. At least I had a dream. When you have dreams, you have a future. I told the manager and his wife, whom I called Mum Coby, that my dream was to continue my studies after high school. They were the best and nicest people I had ever met up to that point in my life.

I finished high school. The Dom girls from my childhood all dropped out of school by the fifth or sixth grade. From my group of Dom girls, only I graduated. Many of them were married by the time they were fifteen or sixteen. At graduation, all the family came and danced together. It was the custom for each student to dance with her family. As we were dancing, we heard, "They are Nawar." We ignored them and enjoyed our dance.

After many months of work, the Dutch couple, Kasie and Coby Veldhuyzen, helped make it possible for me to attend Ibrahimeh College, a private business college, and begin my study of business administration. They helped some financially and gave me flexible working hours so I could take classes.

When Chadra began working at the Dutch guest house, Kasie and Coby did not know she was a Gypsy. They thought she was from the Arab community. They still did not know we were Dom when I started working there. One time they came to my home to visit and saw how simple my home was. It was then that they asked about our background. The way they treated us did not change because they had known us first as hard workers, and only then as Gypsies. They did become very generous to us because they saw how simply we lived.

I lived at home, worked, and went to college. It was a good life. I liked being a student. I liked high school more because I could be myself.

In college, I had to learn to be professional. Still, I had a good time studying. I made many friends in part because I like to speak with people and make jokes.

Being a Gypsy was still difficult. I tried not to talk about it, but I looked different and they knew. During my first year of studies, I met a nice Arab girl. We became good friends. During the New Year vacation, I invited her to my house. When she came to my street, she asked the locals where my house was. They said, "Amoun from the Nawar?"

The next time we met in school, it was obvious that she had changed. She did not talk with me. I asked her if something was wrong. At first, she said no, but then she asked me if I was really a Gypsy. I responded, "Does it matter?"

She said, "Yes."

I said, "Yes, I am a Gypsy and am from the Nawar." From that moment on, I never heard from her again.

One professor during Ramadan, told a story of going to the mosque. He said, "A Nawar woman begged from me." Like many people, he associated anything that happened in the streets with Gypsies. He was angry. I wanted to speak up and say, "I am one of that group," but I didn't have the courage. Later, he discovered that I was Gypsy.

When I was in college, there were good times, too. I was asked to speak about my education in front of forty-five guests from Germany who came to visit my school. Most of my peers did not know how to speak English, so the teacher asked me to come and talk with the guests. Again, my English skills came in handy. I made a small joke about the price of the school, which the head of the school was not happy about, but it helped break the ice.

If the guests asked me personal questions about my background, I changed topics quickly by making jokes—a skill I learned at an early age to deflect hostility towards being a Gypsy.

Also during my first year, I was able to afford things like new clothes, field trips, candy, and school lunches that I could not have as a child. I liked shopping a lot and bought all my own clothes. I started to own things which was unique in my community. Still, I needed to help my family, so I had to set priorities.

I studied at college for three years. I was so thankful to the owners of that Dutch guesthouse for giving me the opportunity to attend college. During my studies in college, I also worked. This important period of my life gave me a push to grow up in nice and good ways. I liked it better than the old ways. The past is good to remember—and also to keep in a special box!

Sadly, in the last year of my studies, the manager of the guest house died two weeks before I received my diploma. Kasie smoked, and he had been coughing since morning. Coby had gone shopping. My sister and I were finishing work before going home. I was preparing the vegetables for the next morning. Kasie said, "I'm going to the little house." It was a place where they had a little privacy behind the guesthouse.

I said, "I will make you some lemonade." When I finished, I took it out and knocked three times as I had been taught. He didn't answer so I began to call. I called and called. Finally, I pushed the door open and saw him lying there. I ran to the house and called the ambulance and called for a man to come help. The man saw that he could not help. The ambulance came within five minutes, but there was nothing they could do.

I was in shock. For a few days, I could not even cry. My father told me I should cry. They all wanted me to come and see him as a corpse, but I did not want to. I wanted to remember him as if he was alive. Until this day, I have a good relationship with his wife and daughter.

It was devastating for me that he would not see me graduate. I wanted to share that day with him. Nevertheless, his wife came and was so happy to see me shine. It meant so much to me that I cried the entire day. All my family and the people who cared about me came, too. I was very happy to be finished with my studies and to start a new life.

CHAPTER FOURTEEN

Adult Adventures

I continued to work at the Dutch guesthouse after I graduated and to meet people from all over the world. I continued to practice my English. I also took training to become a tour guide. I finished the requirements of the Arab area to be a tour guide, but was not able to complete the additional year required by the Israeli government to get the tourist license. It was very expensive. Even though I didn't finish, the education was like a vitamin for me as I learned about all the places in the Holy Land. It helped me to learn how to work with people, which was helpful for my work later. As a worker in a hotel, tourist business is important. I started the two-year course and found a place to sit behind a pillar so I would not be noticed. I planned to learn, not to form relationships.

The teacher asked, "Are you with us?"

I said, "Yes."

"Who are you?"

"Amoun Sleem."

"From?"

"Old City."

He was trying to get my attention. I disagreed with one of his statements about the area. He asked me why, and I said, "Because I live there."

From day to day, we continued in this manner. He would make a statement, and I would disagree. Finally, he asked, "Do you have a problem with me?"

I said, "No, I just know the area because I live there."

After that, I just listened to him and learned more from him than from the book they gave us to study. From the beginning, he felt like I was different. I put distance between us because I was just seeking the learning.

Finally, I said, "I am from the Nawar."

He said, "It's okay. We are all human."

We have been friends ever since, and he has been to my home many times.

While I was still working at the guesthouse, my father had to intervene to stop revenge from turning into a neighborhood war. Rafat, a Gypsy boy of seven, lived inside the Old City. His mom gave him five shekels to get bread. A 20-year-old Arab man caught him and killed him with a knife at his throat. The man was possibly on drugs. People had heard the man say, "I want to kill a Gypsy."

I was working. At the time, cell phones were becoming common and I had one. People kept calling me, but I couldn't find out what really happened.

At the end of the day, I returned to silence at the Lions' Gate. My family was gone. The house was empty. My family had gone to Rafat's house. Everyone was in shock and were gathering together. Finally, someone told me a man had killed Rafat. My feet were frozen.

Rafat used to come to my house to learn with the other kids. He was a simple boy, not very confident. It was hard for him to hold a pencil. I kept telling him he had to try.

The whole community wanted to get revenge. The Arab custom in a situation like this was to burn the person's house or business or maybe kill a member of his family. The Gypsies have taken up some of the Arab ways of dealing with problems.

My father tried to use wisdom for peace. He said the man did the murder, and we need to let the police take care of it. We should not punish those who are not at fault. He said, "Revenge is not for us." This was very unusual in the Middle East. The man was arrested and remains in jail.

I learned to speak Dutch from the managers and their guests as I worked. I made friends with them and received invitations to go visit Holland. After my studies, travel became another dream of mine, but travel was still unheard of for Gypsies in my community, especially for Gypsy women. In my culture, girls do not go places alone—let alone fly far away from home. I knew it would not be easy, but I began to collect money for my first trip out of the country. I told my father about my travel plans. At first, he was not happy, but eventually he gave his permission.

On February 26, 1993, I became the first Gypsy woman in our community to board an airplane. My family and people from my work drove me to the airport. I had a night flight.

When it came time to fly, I became really afraid. I was alone, and it was dark in the airplane. I thought to myself, "What if something happens to the engine and I have to swim in the sea? I do not know how to swim!"

I started to cry, and the man sitting next to me asked if everything was under control. I lied, and said everything was fine. I did not start to feel better until the flight attendants served food and I saw people moving around inside the plane. The man also started to talk to me and told me his story. He was going to visit his mother in Holland. This helped take my mind off my worry about the engine failing. I was happy when we started to descend because I knew we would be on the ground soon. We landed, and my dream came true. I was in Holland, in the green land.

There were people waiting for me at the airport. I had met them when they stayed at the guesthouse where I worked. Dutch people were the most predominant at the hotel. Even though I was tired and wanted to sleep, I talked with them the whole way. We arrived at their house, and my room was on the second floor. It was the first time I had slept far from home, the first time I had slept in a bed off the floor, and the first time to be without my sisters in the room with me. It really felt different when I woke up alone the next morning. It was a strange feeling.

For fourteen days, I spoke only English and Dutch. It was different, hard, and strange, but nice. It was a big step in my life.

I kept the window in my room open in the mornings and watched the street. It was fun to watch the busy people walking by, taking children to school, and doing their shopping. For me, it was special to see.

I felt like a Bedouin who has left his tent for the first time to see the city. Here I was experiencing the same thing. It was my first time outside of Israel, and everything was very different from my little community. I felt strange and afraid to make mistakes. I walked around the village and visited a lot of people, many of whom showed me around the country. I saw so much and liked it so much. Before I knew it, my holiday was over, and I had to get back home.

Flying home was easier because I had done it before. I did not feel afraid. I was welcomed by my entire family, except my father, and by two people from work. I had been homesick in Holland.

When I returned home, I went back to my normal life and decided to save money again for another visit to Holland. This was a strange thing for a Gypsy to do. I asked my brother Ali if he wanted to come with me to Holland.

Ali is nice and a very good friend of mine. He is clever, handsome, and open with people. He does not look Gypsy and has been working on the Jewish side of the city for more than ten years. People like him a lot.

I knew he needed a holiday. So he decided to come with me to Holland. I also asked my sister Zarifeh, who had been working as a nurse for twelve years, if she wanted to come, too. She is the quiet one in the family who likes to help people.

Two or three years later, we three went together to Holland. It was their first time to fly and my second time. We had problems before we even left the airport because we did not have any passports. We only had travel documents because we were Gypsies, not citizens of the country where we live. In the end, we managed to board the plane.

When we arrived in Holland, there was water everywhere, and it was so green. We had fun and spent time shopping for presents to bring back to everyone. My father said the family missed us while we were there because it was so quiet without us. I knew he meant me because I talk too much.

When we returned home, the whole family came to meet us. They made a nice meal for us—a chicken dish with potatoes, vegetables, or rice. During the evening, it was announced that Mohammed decided to get married. It would be the first wedding among the siblings. The big surprise was that he was going to marry an Arab girl. He was twenty-eight years old, and she was twenty-two. She was in college.

CHAPTER FIFTEEN

A New Dream

After the Dutch Guesthouse closed in 2003, I found a small job in a hotel in Jerusalem where I could fix their garden. The garden was an outside restaurant. This was an unusual job for a woman in an Arab area, but I worked without shame because I really love working with plants.

Even before the guesthouse closed, I had begun the work at the Domari Center. The idea of starting a community center for Gypsies first came to me because I wanted a place that would be surrounded by positive thoughts about Gypsy culture. I didn't begin by dreaming big. I started the work in my home, just helping people. There was no salary for this work. Only in recent years have I received a salary. Even now, it is the lowest salary in Jerusalem. I felt useful as I helped people. I was trying something new that I enjoyed.

Even before we had a place called the Domari Center, help began to come from many people and places. I began to get volunteers from all over the world. I felt lucky that God opened doors to many people to come and help. Many of them still have a place in my heart, and I am thankful that I

Varanda of the Sleems' home that was later renovated for the first office and classroom for the Domari Society's programs.

met them and for the great work they did among the children. With many of them, we still have a good relationship.

One of the earliest special people was a woman about sixty years old who helped me with the children. Pat Brown was like a mother for me. We would hang out together to eat or drink something. We liked to go to Ben Yahuda Street for these outings. Pat was one of the first people to say that I should start an organization for this Gypsy work.

In 1998, I had collected some clothing with an American lady named Wendy Ward. She said I should try to find other people to help, so I wrote letters on an old, secondhand computer that I kept under my bed. She contacted Allen and Verr Dean Williams and from that time, we started our journey with the Dom Research Center that continues until this moment.

My relationship with the Williams family started quickly. Our unique friendship started in a strange way. Verr Dean liked the Gypsy dress I had on, and I liked her American dress. We decided to trade. Verr Dean likes to wear her dress and tell this story when she makes talks about Gypsies. She ends with, "Sisters trade clothes. This makes Amoun and me sisters."

Allen and Verr Dean stayed with us like family. They ate our food, listened to our stories, and became close to our hearts. My father said he could tell they were good people when he met them. He could see it in their eyes.

Pat Brown had another idea. She connected me with a Jewish lawyer. Amoun never expected to meet a lawyer! Omri, the lawyer, never knew there were Gypsies in the Middle East. He sat in his ponytail in a big office. Zarifeh and Ali went with me.

He said, "Gypsies?"

I said, "Yeah."

He said, "I didn't know that."

I said, "Here we are. We're trying to make an organization."

He said, "That's hard work."

"I know." My heart was thumping.

He said, "Okay, let's meet Wednesday, and I'll try to get in touch with the office that gives permission."

He called the next day. "Can you come tomorrow?"

Why did he call so soon? I asked Ali to go with me. We got stuck in traffic. Omri kept calling. "Where are you? I have people waiting here in my office to talk to you."

Finally, we got to the office. Anat Hoffman, who was on the Jerusalem city council, was very excited to find there were Gypsies living in Israel. She gave me a big hug because she was happy to meet a Gypsy woman. She offered her services to be on the board of the organization. She had waited an hour. Ever since, when we have a meeting, she always says, "Amoun will be late."

I told Omri I had no money to pay, only my golden necklace from my mother.

He said, "Keep it. When you have money, you can pay."

To this day, I feel I can call him when I need help.

God knows when I need a human to give psychological support. I chanced to meet a great chef who works in a famous hotel here in Jerusalem. Of course, when he wants to say nice words, he uses the words of food and drink. He said, "Amoun, you are like a bottle of wine. Whenever it becomes old, the price is more. The more advanced you become in age, the greater your beauty."

In 2000, we started a nonprofit. We began with courses for women and children. We worked on literacy and job skills. We taught classes in

As the Domari Society's work began, classes for the children were held on the veranda of Amoun's home.

Children's program in the yard of the Sleems' home.

Volunteers making a patio and landscaping the yard after the varanda was renovated for office and classroom space.

Sign outside the Domari Society Community Center.

English and Arabic. I began in my bedroom with an old computer from an American lady, and things stored under my bed. With the computer, I tried to reach people all over the world. In the beginning, my goal was to bring change to my community and to change the attitudes of people toward the Gypsies.

Our house was open for people to see. I wanted to let them see what was behind the door, to see that we were clean with nothing to shame us. In fact, Gypsy people have strict rules about cleanliness, especially with food preparation. We must clean our chicken with olive oil, fresh lemon, and salt.

I was following family tradition. We were the first family to be open to outsiders. My grandmother and my mother welcomed tourists walking along the wall and asked them in for tea. Many were from the United Nations and worked in Jerusalem because of trouble along the Lebanese border. In later years after their assignment was finished and they had returned to their home countries, they would come back to visit.

For four years, the work was in my home in my bedroom. When we had more students, we moved outside on the veranda. In winter, which lasts about six months, we could not meet because of the weather. Children came to my home to learn ABCs or to read and write. Volunteers helped in my backyard. They taught the little ones so they would be ready for school and the dropouts so they could drop back in.

In 2002, funds were given through the Dom Research Center to add an office and classroom space. We closed in the veranda to make a warm room. We got tables, chairs, and financial help to get the Center started officially. We were open for people to come in. Volunteers came from Jerusalem College and other areas, mostly from America. The neighbors complained that the children were noisy. I had no privacy with so many people coming to visit. I was concerned that the Arab neighbors would be nervous with so many people coming to the house.

Allen Williams found groups willing to send food and blankets. Then we had a food and blanket distribution. A huge number of people came to my home. Some got mad about how much each got, and some came back after the distribution was over asking for more. Blankets almost covered the whole community, but whatever we had was never enough. My father was nervous about the attitude of the people, and also about the problems this could create with the neighbors. The next food distribution was not at my home. We moved it to the Lions' Gate.

We had no building so we gave them out from a place on the street at the Lions' Gate. In this way, we began some of the programs to help people in the community.

I felt like a Bedouin with no tent of my own. I said, "God, I need a roof over my head." I brought my sadness to Allen Williams. He said we needed to have a place. We worked together and tried to build a building, but it did not work. We thought we would build a prefabricated building in the garden next to our home. Building in the Old City is complicated with many filings for permits with many different groups. Sometimes, it is hard to know who gets to give approval. We hired a contractor who knew about filing permits. We took a big setback when the contractor suddenly quit answering our calls and took the money that had been given him for the permits. It was a discouraging time.

One day I was with my sister Zarifeh on the bus. A man came to her and asked her if she knew someone who would like to rent a place in the area of Shuafat. The place was fifteen minutes from my home. God was matching me. For three hours on the bus, I sat dreaming, hoping it was the answer for me.

The money we had for the building became the money for rent. The rent was $600. I called Allen. We had enough money on hand for two years.

From that time, everything went smoothly. It was like the space was looking for ones called Gypsy. We collected things. We found thrown-away furniture, fixed it up, and now it is beautiful. We had a grand opening.

Volunteers helped me write grant requests to support our programs. We learned that organizations don't like to pay for salaries and overhead costs. Much of that is paid for by individual supporters of the center.

Caral Miller from Canada has helped the Center from the heart with what she has. Many times she gives food for the Center and also speaks to other people about the center.

Dafna Strauss is one of our board members. She helps with paperwork, especially the ones for the government.

Dom bazaar held at the Hebrew Union College.

Ariela Marshall volunteered almost from the beginning. Her behavior was almost more Gypsy than me. We were more like sisters. We built our dream together, and she knew what I wanted to have. She is one of the real people who never give up on us.

Stephanie, from Germany, was in Jerusalem with her husband who worked for his government. She wanted something to do, and her friend told her about the center. She volunteered often. I remain friends with her family. I may wake up and see a bag of chocolate from this good friend. It pleases me, and it pleases the kids in my home. She may bring her three children for lunch at the Domari Center. It is so lovely to see three German children playing with the Gypsy kids.

Sometimes one friend leads to another. Allen Williams knew about my dream to write my story to bring understanding about the Gypsy people. He knew Virginia Butler, a writer who was willing to help. For months, I answered her questions by Facebook message. Then Allen and Verr Dean helped me arrange a trip to the United States and took me to her home in Mississippi. Sometimes you meet people for the first time, and you get that great feeling like you have known them for many years. I believe God matches people together, and that's what happened when I met this woman who helped me write my story without knowing me. For two days, we sat at her dining room table. Allen would suggest a story he remembered, and I would tell that one. Then Virginia asked for more stories and more details. She drove me crazy, but in a good way, like I did with the Father at St. Anne's church.

CHAPTER SIXTEEN

Savoring Successes

At the same time that people were coming into our lives, God was matching us with many good activities. We've had catering courses for women three times, sewing two times, hair dressing one time, cosmetics one time, healthcare lectures for young mothers, and an afterschool tutoring program for four years. Women make traditional Gypsy handicrafts to sell. One of the most beautiful is the traditional colored pillow the bride's mother makes for her to give her good sleep. We hope to bring back some of those beautiful traditions here at the Domari Center. Some of these handicrafts are sold at the good hotels where there is pride in the high quality of Gypsy work.

The healthcare lectures are very important since Gypsies marry at a young age and have children very young. By the time a woman is twenty years old she may have five children. The lectures educate the mothers about their bodies and about childbearing. They learn how to give time between the babies and how to care for the children. Many of the women have listened and are doing better.

We have successful Gypsy bazaars each year with food, hand embroidery, jewelry, scarves, soaps (the olive oil soap of my childhood days), children's clothes, knitting, and crochet. I feel that these bazaars have been good experiences for me and for the women who made the crafts.

Graduation for Women's Catering Class, 2004.

We received a lot of good attention from people. The first bazaar was in 2000 at the Hebrew College. We've had one every year since then at places like the American Colony Hotel, Notre Dame Center, Jerusalem Hotel, and also at many craft fairs, guest houses, and churches.

Even though some people came just to see what level we had reached. Many people were impressed with the work we could do. You could see on the faces of others that we were still on the way and needed to improve, but I was happy with the point we had reached. We were standing on our own feet before the world. Each bazaar was nicer than the one before, and we never repeated ourselves.

Some people from a residential home for the elderly visited the center. The people from the residential home are Jewish. They began coming to the center in 2012, and now they come two or three times a year. They loved the center and did some shopping. I must say I am the old lady, not them. One lady wanted the really big Gypsy earrings. Thinking that when we are old our ears are not like when we are young, I tried to push her to some simple ones, not the heavy earrings. But this lady had confidence, and she only wanted that heavy design. I put them in her ears and hoped they would not pull her ears down. She gave me a good lesson. If you want and believe in something, you should do it even if it costs you pain.

We are often invited to a large exhibition with several colorful tables of Gypsy crafts by several people who love our work. We enjoy seeing other organizations that come from over the country to sell their work. We enjoy woman talk and seeing people who visited with us from last year. I hope this year will be even better than last year so our women can be proud of their work. For people who make bad stories about Gypsies, they should read this and know that we are people who work hard for a living.

In afterschool programs, we support children with homework because their parents may not be able to read and write. We encourage them to have dreams of the jobs they would like to have rather than just thinking of how they can survive.

Prejudice in schools is not as bad as when I was a child, but there are still problems. My niece came to me complaining. Every time the kids from her classroom do anything naughty, the teacher says, "All of you are like Gypsy people." My niece asked me if we could choose another nationality. That made me sad.

I said, "We need to change the teacher, not our nationality. You should be proud of yourself. You should keep being a good student. We are Gypsy with a great heart and a love of all kinds of nations."

I wrote about one instance on Facebook. Two girls had not found any place in school for the year. The doors were closed, and they faced losing a year of school. I took that as a challenge. The message of the Domari Center is "a place for everyone and the first educated generation." After I wrote this publicly, social workers in Jerusalem became worried that this word would get out and found a place for the two girls.

When the kids are having examinations at the end of the school year, the Center has an Emergency Period. We work like crazy to get them to pass with great marks. I stay optimistic that we will get great certificates from many kids. I sometimes feel like an old lady tired from everyday work, but in many ways I feel like I am Superwoman who never gives up on the strong side of me.

We got one of the most beautiful certificates from one of the kids who received our support with education at the Domari Center. He was chosen to be one of the best students in the school. I am definitely proud, and it gives me a push to keep going with the future of a more educated generation. We have more and more successful stories from kids at the Domari Center from their schools. People open their hands to the afterschool tutoring programs and make this Domari dream a great success! We give thanks for the friends of the Domari who are always there for these kids.

As the school year ends, I do some small shopping for the kids who made this year a success. I feel that all the pressure and energy we put into the program had meaning and gave great returns. We make a dream come true for some of them. They want to go to the sea. We plan a trip for them and their families together to go to the sea. I wish I could take my entire community, but I have to go with my ability. I am proud in my heart and full of the love of God in my heart for the people.

The Domari Center is like a beehive that gives good honey. The kids study and work, and Amoun cleans around them. The children keep us smiling.

Sometimes with all that goes on, I feel like a woman standing alone. But I have a sweet army. Most of them are women and kids. I may have three meetings with women on a busy morning. I love these women's meetings. I always discover who loves to be active and practical and who wants to just take things easy. Some are women lionesses who cross me, but I learn from them and am happy with the meeting. My father was right when he said, "This life is a big school, and every day you learn something." I'm glad I'm still learning. These are women who make great change in this world.

With this sweet army of women and kids, we handle the Center and face our difficulties. One small smile from a kid gives me a great push to stand with amazing confidence.

One morning, I sat close to three kids and listened to their conversation. Younah and Yousef are brother and sister, and Sarah is a cousin. Younah said, "Yousef, you like Sarah more than me."

Yousef answered, "Yes, you are my sister so I can't marry you, but I can marry Sarah."

What smart Gypsy kids!

One of our little girls took an exam. The teacher told her that her parents must sign the paper. She brought it back the next day signed "Mom" and "Dad." The paper was not bad. She was just taking care of it herself.

I follow the story of two young men growing up in this area. I love their friendship. They are three-year-old cousins, Omar and Adam. Whatever you give to one, the other will say, "And to my friend." Even their mothers face the same problem when it's nighttime, they need to sleep close to each other or they keep crying. Their Gypsy love and good roots based on sharing would make a message to old people who don't understand the meaning of good friendship.

We have a strict policy here at the center that there is no difference in the boys and girls. Everyone must help with the cleaning and organizing things that have been used. One day, I went to close the window and heard two boys talking to each other. "Let's go slowly before Shrek sees us and makes us clean."

I was a little bit mad, but I smiled at the same time. I like Shrek. I called them and said, "Shrek wants you to clean, Sweet Faces." I wish you could have seen their faces. Now I have a new name—Amoun Shrek. What must I say—Gypsy boys!

I don't think I am a bad person to make the kids at the center put things in order. I teach them there is a time to work and a time to play according to their age. They receive, but they can also give. I learned this way from my grandmother, and right now, I am more than thankful that she always pushed me to learn. We kids and adults must keep our door open to anyone who gives us ways to learn.

We started one morning in the kitchen making apple cake. The day before we had made banana cake and thought we were through for the day, but the kids finished it off. I call them the Shrek kids. This day we decided to be smart and make it before they came. They love the sweet cakes—and chocolate. I hope their lives will be sweet, too.

One kid asked, "Hi, miss, what are you going to cook for us now?"

I answered him with a pretend angry face, "No food. We have a strike today."

He said, "You have no hospitality like our house. You are not a Gypsy woman."

I was proud of how he was raised and decided I should start cooking. Otherwise, I would be the story of the city.

I thought I was a clever person and hid the chocolate where not even a mouse could find it, but my Sweet Faces showed me I was stupid. There are no secret places at the Domari Center.

They also love pencils. Whenever I put a pencil on my desk, their magic fingers come and take it. They must think I am a pencil factory.

These clever Gypsy children know the timing of the hunter. When they see you are busy, they move so slowly like a tiger. They use everything you say "no" to, tamper with things, and eat like crazy. I do play cat and mouse with the Domari kids. They drive me crazy, but they make me smile inside.

Sometimes they are like monkeys coming to the center in very bad weather. They say, "We need to study." It makes me very proud of the courage we build in the Dom kids. I see hope in the new generation. It's not bad at all to be Gypsy.

Recently, I traveled to the United States to work with those who are helping me tell my story. When I returned after a two-week absence, the kids in my home welcomed me in a way that made me want to cry. When I sat to eat on the floor, they sat around me in a circle like we were playing a game. The next morning when I woke up, Adam woke up, too. He said, "I am going with you," and he woke up his cousin Omar. They stood watching me like an army. When I went to take my shower, they stood near the door—a Gypsy Army. I'm glad God is giving me this love. What do I need more?

It is a blessing to me to hear a child who is not yet two call my name and want to be around me. I feel like a mom with all these kids around even though I am not. For sure, it is a rich feeling, and I give thanks to God.

Recently men have come to the center wanting to learn to read and write. They want to come only on Saturday when no one else is there. Saturday is their day off, but also they are ashamed. They gave me orders about when and where the classes were to be. Eight men come every Saturday. One wants to know how to write "I love you," to his wife. Some had not wanted me to continue with this program in the past because I was a woman.

The men say women are difficult, but I must say that is not the truth. When men sit together, they are worse than women. They talk all the time without stopping. Their teacher told me, "For sure my hair will get gray, and I will dye my hair after one month."

I say, "So if you want to dye your hair, just come to the Domari Center, and you can choose the color you want." Poor teacher.

I had been waiting a long time and going through many difficulties with the men against me. Then came the day when one of the men asked, "Can I make you coffee?"

In my heart, I said, "Wow, that is a big change! I usually make coffee for them, and now they do it for me."

I saw the truth of the saying, "Every day is a new day," on the morning of the men's test in the literacy course. The Domari men had their alphabet exam. Their faces—so serious, no laughing, no smiling—I wish you could see. They were just writing as if the teacher was punishing them. But all of this is Top Secret. No strangers can see them until they can write a letter. I love to see them working hard.

I feel great that change has started to move. So many of us are giving our lives for our belief in the work we do. I wish my dad was alive to see how many of the goals we have reached.

Gypsies from the West Bank came in grief when my father died. We had been doing traditional handicrafts to see for about a year. Shortly after my father's funeral one of the women said to me, "You should be giving us attention because you are one of us." She insisted that I come and visit to see their work. They think I have my nose high, but it is flat.

I knew I needed to travel to the West Bank to meet some families. I was very tired and busy. I would lie if I said I had the energy, but sometimes you need to do what you should do. They are my people and when they are in need, I have to show up.

Once a week for a year, I visited. I brought second-hand clothes, money for their crafts, and food. I ate with them. I bought their stuff and sold it with the ones from the Domari Center. Now they think my nose is flat.

They are very skilled in designed handicrafts. When I tell them about a new design, they say, "Oh, that's easy. We've done that before."

After one visit, I wrote on Facebook, "I never felt more joyful in my life than when I visited these Dom people in the West Bank. They have a simple life, living in nature, with hospitality for others. Even with its difficulties, they find ways to be joyful and have peace in their everyday living. They made us a great meal that I enjoyed more than a five-star restaurant, made more delicious with love. It made me rest and almost sleep." The meal was *maqluba*, a traditional dish, that means upside down rice and chicken with two kinds of vegetables.

They love to share this hospitality. When I took a tour with visiting Holland Gypsy families to the West Bank, I was proud of their hospitality.

Crafts on display at the Domari Society Community Center, 2013.

Crafts on display at the Domari Society Community Center, 2013.

Some of the dresses made by the Dom women in the sewing program at the Domari Society Community Center.

Even without notice that we were coming, their door was open. They welcomed the guests, shared their food, and made them feel at home.

The women came to visit me through the dangerous occupied zone with a heavy checkpoint. Not even a bird can enter without going through the checkpoint. They came through the bypaths and forest. They arrived with burrs stuck to their long black dresses.

They really want to be at the Center. They relax with one another and breathe freely. They are making some money from their sewing. Some of the younger women like to see their craziness and creativity with the jewelry. In one village, there are now twenty-five women working with the handicraft program.

One evening I received a phone call from a Dom woman on the West Bank. Usually they ring once, and I get back to them. She had a strange request. "Amoun, I need you to get me a computer."

I know she is not that good at reading and writing. I asked her why.

She said, "I need to learn and work on my skills. I signed up for the course in knitting wool. The lady who gave the course kicked me out because I came with my baby. I need to see the new designs. I know I can do them, and through the Internet, I can learn."

She is the best I have in knitting wool. This is a story of self-determination showing how this woman wants to survive. I respect her so much. I'm just afraid she will ask me next time to start wearing pants, and her husband will come shoot me down.

I wish they lived close to me because it is so hard to get here from the checkpoint, but I am sure we can make a difference. We will be number one in designs because when God gives a talent, it is different from learning it. For sure, the Domari Center is a place for everyone, no matter if you are here or there.

A Dom boy on the West Bank left me sleepless. I prayed that God would lead me to people who would help him. He is seventeen years old and has grown just three teeth in his mouth. He finds it hard to smile and stays at home. Working with the Dom Research Center, we have found help for this boy. By the time this book is published he should have teeth and a smile on his face. Already he is thinking about the future and asks his mother to find him a wife. I tell him, "First get your teeth, then think about a wife."

CHAPTER SEVENTEEN

Telling the Gypsy Story

When I started the Domari Society, I wanted people to know my community and see it differently. I wanted change for my community and change in the way people looked at us. I've told my stories personally and in newspapers, magazines, interviews, and on the Internet. In 2000 some of my stories were put on the Internet in the *Kuri Journal* by the Dom Research Center. In 2001, many stories of my community were written in a book called *The Dom of Jerusalem: A Gypsy Community Chronicle*. With all these stories, my dream was to help other people see the hard life of the Gypsies and the beautiful parts that we live. Our dances, musicians, and special clothes show our culture. There have been Gypsy people who helped Arab people with songs and stories. I want people to know our place and what we give to society.

The articles and stories created interest about the Gypsies in the land. Opportunities for spoken and written words about the Gypsy community come more often. I cannot say the interest was always good for us, maybe 50/50.

Release of *The Dom of Jerusalem: A Gypsy Community Chronicle* with the Dom Research Center, 2001.

The organization called Domari: the Society of Gypsies in Israel began at the end of 1999 to support the causes and needs of the Gypsy people. They asked me to speak at the opening.

I was nervous about making a speech in front of many people. Even though people think I'm strong, I'm like a little child afraid to make mistakes in front of people.

Amoun's Speech

November 23, 1999 at Opening of the Domari Society

Good evening friends. We are here tonight to celebrate a new beginning. A new beginning for my people, the Gypsies.

If you know anything about Gypsies, you know that they are a people who have been discriminated against throughout their long history. They have moved from country to country in order to be at peace with others.

My people (forefathers) have lived in the Old City of Jerusalem and the West Bank for over 100 years, and yet, in many ways, during these 100 years our standard of living and status of life has not changed. Many of my people still live without electricity. Many do not have indoor plumbing. Many cannot read or write.

When I was a child I was fortunate to be able to go to school. But we had no electricity at home and I, as well as my brothers and sisters, had to do my homework in the evening by candlelight.

We were discriminated against in school by the teachers and classmates. I saw at that time that there were many things that needed to be changed if my people were going to be accepted and given the opportunities that all other people have.

Today we have electricity in our home. Through hard work and perseverance we were able to change this situation. And I believe we can do this for my community as well.

People say that dreams can come true. I believe this is true. And because you are here tonight, you also believe this. Together, side by side, we can make OUR dream a reality.

What are the goals of this new organization, the Domari Society of Gypsies?

We would like to raise our standard of living through education and health care.

Many of the Gypsy children do not attend school because they are discriminated against by the teachers and other students. Many are ashamed to go to school because they do not have clothes or backpacks like the other children. Because their parents did not attend school, they are unable to get good jobs and don't have the money needed to buy the books and school supplies.

If the children were to attend school, they would be able to get better jobs and raise their standard of living.

Health care is another concern of our organization. We need to teach the women how to care for the health of their children and family. We need to look at how we can help the disabled in our community. Currently, there is no health care available in our community. This needs to be changed.

My people have waited for this day for many years. Many of them have given up because they believe that no one cares about the Gypsies. All they know and remember is that throughout history many people tried to kill the Gypsies. Their homes were burned down and they were forced to flee from place to place. Why? What is their crime? They are Gypsies.

We are here today to say "Stop!" We know that God created all men equal. With the establishment of this organization we want to give hope to my people, the Gypsies. Thank you, all of you, for standing with me. Many of you know that it has taken many years for my dream—our dream—to come true. We still have a long way to go. But I know if we work together, side by side, we can make this dream a reality.

Thank you,
Amoun Sleem

I still get nervous when I have to make a speech. I think if I become 100 years old this nervousness will still be inside me. Still, I speak whenever I am asked in order to tell our story.

Someone at a lecture told me, "Your English is quite good," in front of about twenty people. "Where did you learn it from?"

I answered, "From the street, sir."

His face became very red, like I was not being respected. This man did not know that I was not born with a golden spoon in my mouth. I was real and picked up my English from selling tourists postcards from an early age. The street was a good school for me and taught me a lot about right and wrong. I did not come from Cambridge University, but it was a five-star university.

In 2002, I received an honor from a foundation in Sweden for my work with the Dom people. Each year this foundation recognizes one person for their humanitarian work. I traveled to Sweden to receive the award. This made me very happy and encouraged me in my work.

Some of the periods I have gone through since the Society began are funny, and I will remember them all my life. I was invited to speak at the meeting of the Gypsy Lore Society in 2003. The meeting was held in New York. I was young and had no idea what academic people thought. I went to the stage and spoke about the Gypsies in the Middle East. When it came to the questions, one professor stood and asked, "How do the Gypsies wash their clothes?"

Without thinking, I answered him, "What a stupid question! Of course, they will wash black with black and white with white." I've never seen people laugh like they laughed. I think the man was asking something different. I'm not sure if this professor was the stupid one or if it was me.

Recently I was invited to speak about Jerusalem at an event run by the American Academy in Jerusalem. The speakers were doctors, filmmakers, academy people, and me, the simple Amoun. I did enjoy what they said about Jerusalem very much. Then it came my turn to talk about Jerusalem. In my simple way, I said, "Maybe you know about Jerusalem from her cultural ways, but I know her in an emotional way. Jerusalem is like my mother where I cannot compare her love to another. Every day that I enter one of her gates, I feel blessed and newborn. I was born, grew up, and still live inside that wall. I will never give up this right."

Interest in the Domari Center is growing outside the Gypsy community. A journalist called for a television interview. I asked him "What kind of story and what kind of questions?" He said there would be all kinds, including political questions. I see more important things than politics. There is a real story about real people who need attention and help. They are everywhere in this world, and they are the Gypsy people.

There have been many journalists who have written articles about me and the Center. Some journalists have been friendly and reported the truth. Some took advantage of my work and of the Gypsy people. They wanted to tell a story that would sell magazines and papers. Others wrote stories that actually hurt me and my community.

One journalist wanted to write a story about the Gypsy people. He went to a famous man and asked how to reach me to write his story. The man said, "Man, the Gypsies are not worth a story." I would say to him, "We are worth and worth and worth. We are people God created, and we love people. Our hearts are full of love for each other. One day these words of racism will disappear forever." The good part is the journalist found me and wrote the story. He was glad to visit our center. I continue to hope that there will be people who will help others understand the Gypsy world.

Alhurra TV came to the Domari Center to report on the Gypsy culture. We are glad to see so many interested in this culture. It is rich in history and has great roots. We are proud of the Domari Center that tries to promote Gypsy history to the world.

The online digital magazine *Your Middle East* carried a feature about our community called, "The Domari of Jerusalem: A Forgotten Community," and Edmund Sanders of *The Los Angeles Times* interviewed me for an article, "In Jerusalem, Activist Hopes to Restore Gypsy Pride."

For a long time, the *Ha'aretz* newspaper wanted to visit our center to do an article on Gypsy food. I told our women, "You can make it. Let's show the world our food." So two women worked together. The newspaper reporter said she approved. She said Gypsy spices were some of the greatest she had ever tasted. Her article featured Bahra, describing how she made *maqluba* and the dumplings called *danan al aut* (cat's ears in the Gypsy language).

She explained to her readers that reservations for lunch can be made by small groups or tourists or anyone wanting to learn the Gypsy culture. So, the next time you are in Jerusalem, don't forget to come eat lunch at the Domari Center. The delicious food featured in *Ha'aretz* made me officially hungry!

In 2002 we made a cookbook after we had catering classes at the Notre Dame Center. The cookbook showed the important part food plays in our culture. We included a section on how the Dom use herbs and spices as natural remedies.

Deborah Ellis, a Canadian writer, has become interested in the children and their hopes and dreams. Even as I write these stories from my life and about the Community Center, Deborah is writing a children's book about the lives of Gypsy children in Jerusalem. The children are happy with her, and she feels right at home. I fix her Gypsy food and hope she enjoys it.

CHAPTER EIGHTEEN

Overcoming Difficulties

We have had our difficulties. My father never looked for power or leadership. As his daughter, I don't look for it either. I did not seek the pain of being a Gypsy, the pain of being a woman, or the pain of people attacking me.

One man has fought the program all the years since our official opening in 2000. His wife is the one who would have taken my gifts of food from the tourist on the bus when I was eight. His life problem is called Amoun. He doesn't know a bigger power surrounds me—God's power.

Whatever I say, he says the opposite. Whenever something good is said about the Center, he tries to destroy it. If I went right, the man went left. He was gambling against me that the center would fail. He put an ad in the paper that this woman was trying to change the Gypsy culture. Now his son is doing the same. For thirteen years, I complained to my father. My father said, "Ignore him."

The program is not popular with some people who see Gypsies as hopeless. Other people get distracted. I was in a meeting with some who call themselves society women. The planned topic was the problems of women. After half an hour, it shifted to Michelle Obama's haircut. I wanted to say, "There are more important things than her haircut. Let us be thinking positively about helping and creating good things for people who need it." I would have been better off staying with my family and drinking tea.

Sometimes people just don't do what they say. Twice, leaders from Europe said they were visiting Jerusalem and said they wanted to visit the Gypsy Center. They never showed up.

Many say I am a strong woman or a woman with strong action. I would lie if I said that I am always a strong woman. Sometimes my balance shakes. Not long after I returned from my trip to the United States, the owner of our Center sold it to a new man. He visited the Center without notice and said, "I am the new owner, and I want to raise the rent."

With Gypsy confidence, I said, "I will not pay one coin more."

Even as my heart is in pain, God shows the strong side of me, and I remember my grandmother Amina who said, "Whoever falls from the sky, the land will receive." So don't worry about the future. In the end, you will see what happens.

The man used all my energy. I felt alone meeting these challenges, and I missed my dad and my strong grandmother. The next morning, I said to myself, "Amoun, when you were a child and afraid of something, you ran to the mountain near your home." These challenges mean that our Center lives day by day.

For the first time in my life, I was glad the week had ended. So many things going on and so many issues to take care of, that I felt my life did not belong to me. There are many who share the same life, but the drama and action make your life special and unique. Sometimes we don't choose the life we want. We are born and suddenly the map is there to start. The choice was God's choice, not ours.

Even the rent increase was not the end. One morning we entered the Domari Center to see that vandals had stolen the hope from the kids. We had been robbed. The landlord tried to raise the rent. It was a wound in the heart of the center. They stole the money from selling jewelry, the silver jewelry, three laptops the kids used for learning, and the kids camera. My heart was in pain. I never understand people who hurt other people. We lost most of our things that we had worked so hard to have because we needed them. I wrote about it on Facebook through my tears.

Sometimes God sends you a message or sign from a person you would never expect to bring you a message. In moments when you feel alone and all the doors seem like they are closed, that person can tell you that you are in God's heart and He cares about you. Sarah, six years old, saw me sitting alone. She came to me and said, "Smile, Aunt Amoun, God loves you!" I saw the great smile on her face. God always knows the right moment to pull you up.

The Domari Center was like a baby who was everything to me. The baby went through good and bad times, but I hoped he would grow up to be a strong baby. I gave him so much of my time and put him inside my heart. I tried to bring his beautiful picture to the world, to share his sadness and happiness, to try to get more people to understand his life. Here today, the baby needs a new bed, a bed he can put all his dolls in so he can play more and have more speed. I believe in God's timing and God's timing shows us that need for change and a move.

We found a nice place, which was bigger than the first center. It has additional room for taking more kids and having a workshop for women separate from the kids. We will be able to cover more Dom people. This was the strong feeling God put inside me. He opened that door and put the light in the end of the tunnel.

Going through this difficult time, I just became more willing to continue the work. So we started something new. We created a new Facebook page of Gypsy food with Gypsy recipes. It is our way to tell all that we trust God in His work.

My friend Rena Lauer, who wrote the Gypsy cooking article in the *Haaretz Digital Edition*, posted the news about the robbery on Facebook and asked for donations. We had so many donations and good wishes that I didn't know how to start to reply. I just sent deep love and thanks to all who helped and promised to go on and never stop dreaming my Gypsy dream.

Moving time! I woke up in the morning feeling like I had stones in my back from the hard work on the new place. Sometimes I wish I had ten hands to finish everything. We still need men's hands to help. Women are women and men are men.

I brought the turtles to the new center and put them outside the veranda. We have a door through to the office. You may believe this or not, but this turtle knocks at the office door and says, "Ms. Sleem, we feel you are very busy, but we are here. Don't forget our breakfast."

Petra van der Zande posted on Facebook soon after the move, "Yesterday we visited Amoun, my Gypsy sister. Her center moved to a new place—beautiful!"

At times you wish to have a new door, a door that doesn't make you feel like you are alone in a room. You need a room full of people, real people who will stand by you in your time of need. Sometimes it takes a while to realize you have to give up on things you love to keep. To understand that maybe can give us peace and be good for us. There will always be another side in this world.

CHAPTER NINETEEN

Jerusalem, My Home

Nothing is more beautiful than my hometown, Jerusalem. Every day I understand why my grandfather and my father lived in the same place for over 200 years. Behind the great walls of Jerusalem, they found that simple life.

My morning walk in the Old City of Jerusalem has a beautiful magic you can feel when you stand by her walls. One morning in December, I watched the old man who sold bagels to everyone enter the Damascus Gate, and I remembered where my father used to sit nearby.

Almost every morning I take one or two three-year-old boys to the center so they can learn and spend time together. Even in cold bad weather, they want to come. It costs me time and makes me walk slowly to my work, but I believe sometimes the smallest things you do become the biggest things, which you can see when you know you have a part in these kids' hearts.

I love coming early in the morning to the Center with everything looking like it is waiting—the flowers for water, the birds and turtles for their food, and the men and women for the new day and new skills. I see peace in

Amoun Sleem and her good friend Ariela Marshall.

great spirits full of love and action. I pray daily that this will continue and more hands will be open to keep this Center going.

One day Jerusalem has cold windy rain, and the street is almost empty. The next day, you wake up and you see a sunny lovely day and say, "It's a blessed land." Then snow comes in a beautiful white dress. People stay home like there's a curfew or a war. The next day when the sun comes out, they are out walking around doing their shopping like nothing happened. God's blessing of rain and snow has come after a long time of waiting for water. This year we will have great fruit and the best extra virgin olive oil. I have always been sure Jerusalem was a blessed land. Spring will bring out the sleeping turtles. They will get their first meal at the Domari Center, a place for everyone. Welcome back!

Then comes summer in Jerusalem. You put the egg outside, and you come back in a few minutes, it is ready to eat! It is so hot, I am almost walking sleeping. A good decision tells the children to stay by their moms. They have the summer activities, playing all the time without stopping with their big energy. They forget that Aunt Amoun is getting to be an old lady, but you know what? That is my joy to see them happy, and I wish I could do even more to bring happiness into their lives.

While the kids are in the summer program, the women have their catering lesson. My sister Amar loves to come to the catering course. This course is the only reason for her to get out of the house. She loves to work with the kitchen chef. She has good taste in cooking so the cooking course gives her confidence and support. I am proud of her and women like her. I am also proud of the Domari Center that gives an opportunity to those who have never been outside their homes before. The women do really good work and the smell from the cooking makes it hard to focus on my work. Visitors are always welcome to come and try our food.

Fall brings warm days for collecting olives from the trees. People stop in lines to drink the fresh juice from the Jericho oranges. This land has been blessed with many gifts God has given to her—weather, food, and holy places.

Friday is Amoun's day—my day off. I walk wherever I want. I love to see the people as I shop for my family. I like to see the routine walking through the Old City in rain or hot weather. I do my shopping, buying fresh vegetables and fruit for my family. I hear the high voice of the old man who sells Jerusalem bread. Tourists may think, "What a terrible voice," but I know it's normal for my city. I fill my eyes with beautiful places I used to go as a child and smile inside. The places remind me how I was a troublemaker, but in a good way. I see all kinds of people and feel the beautiful spirit of the city. I thank God for making my home here.

A man may stop me on my morning walk and say, "I love your spirit." I see him selling on the street every day and say, "Good morning." We have never talked before. It makes me remember my father saying, "Better days are coming, in God's will."

I go to buy fabric, and the man says, "You drive me crazy with all these colors. You are like Gypsy people. They love crazy and strong colors."

He made me smile. I said to him, "Believe me. I am Gypsy. Nothing is better than being Gypsy."

I have a tradition for many years of doing one thing every Friday. It is a habit that I love and would not find it easy to change. I like the Jewish tradition. Every Friday in each street in Jerusalem, there is a boy or man sitting here or there, selling flowers. I believe every Jewish man likes to get flowers for his wife on Friday. But me—no man, no husband. I make a husband for myself. I buy flowers for myself. I like to put them in our room and share them with my sisters.

Honestly, sometimes I drive the man who sells the flowers crazy, because I try to get one flower from each box and mix it together. This man is used to my face, and he became nice to me and let me choose the ones I like. But sometimes I drive him crazy because I want every one to be perfect. He starts to shout at me and says, "Dai!" in Hebrew. That means, "Leave it."

Afterwards when these flowers start to wilt, it is time for Amoun's hands to come and pick them up and dry them. I dry as many flowers as I can each week. The entrance to my home is full of many different beautiful dried flowers.

I mentioned to my good friend Ariela Marshall that my dream is to have my own flower store because I believe that is my world, and I love to be around them.

Back at home, we still have the system that my father grew inside us. We must eat as a family—kids, mother, sisters, and brothers. It can drive you crazy with all the kids talking through the meal, but it's really like you put extra spices on the food. My dad knew what was best for the family.

Every Friday my father wanted the family to have breakfast together since everyone was at home and not working on that day. Everyone prepared something like white cheese, bagels, hummus, tomatoes, olives, cucumbers, and omelets. We sat on the floor with the food in the middle. We still do this breakfast. Everyone talks together and enjoys food and family conversation. The tradition started from my father's parents. My father said eating alone is not a pleasure, but eating with someone brings joy. I remember doing this even as a small child but the food was simpler then—eggs, garlic, tomatoes with Gypsy spices. The dish is called *shackshukeh*. This was a big dish feeding eight or nine people and was cooked in a very large dish. We drank hot tea with it. Even the teapot was large so that they didn't have to keep making more. The company was good, the food was delicious. Since my Father's death, the children and their families continue this tradition, eating the meal outside under the grape vines.

On Saturdays, I go outside Jerusalem to a place near Jericho where some Gypsies work in a flower stall by the road. I go there every Saturday and try to help them. In the end, the man offers me one small plant, or if I have enough money, I buy one or two plants. That's why in our home we have a lot of beautiful plants and a feeling of being in great beauty. My second place is my Domari Center where we have beautiful plants everywhere. What can I do? I'm a nature lover like my grandmothers.

I appreciate the people and know the value of the city with treats for the eyes as soon as you enter just one gate of the city. We run the Center the same way, peacefully and with great visitors always around. We trust God in our work and never pass a day without people around us. We love that great spirit, our visitors, and those who have served our people. This is my place now. I know that God made his map for me! This is my home!

CHAPTER TWENTY

Still Dreaming

Today, I try to live my life with what we call "walking straight," so I do not bring disrespect to the two cultures of my community, the Arabs and the Gypsies. I don't understand all that God brought me through since I was a child. I know He wanted me to build myself and prepare for the difficulties I see as a Dom woman. I felt it was a great school. I learned to work with kids, visitors, phone calls, and interviews all at the same time with people working all around me. I learned to smile, to cry, to love, to forgive, and to go on with this world in order to survive. In the end, God is the great teacher.

I see discrimination still. Not long ago I was invited to the home of my friend for a meal the day before her son got married. She is from a high society family. I didn't feel like going, but she is a friend, so I went. The house was full of prestigious people and I felt like, "Wow, I made a mistake."

I went in but felt like everyone was looking at me. I felt special—that is different—because I was dark. I felt like a Bedouin entering the city for the first time. Many gathered around asking where I was from. When I told them

Amoun Sleem modeling clothing made by Dom women at the Community Center, 2012.

I was from the Old City, they knew I was from the Gypsy people. Some were talking and pointing. Some of their looks were asking, "What is she doing here?" It was a very uncomfortable time. I went and sat outside the middle of the group. Finally, I left without lunch. My friend saved my lunch and gave it to me the next day. She understood my discomfort.

Even though I have written about the problems within my community, I am very much connected to my heritage emotionally and in my soul. It is not an easy culture, but I believe in the good things in my society. I believe Gypsies should have respect for other people even if that respect is not returned. We are flexible and try in simple ways to make ourselves fit in with other cultures. We do not talk about politics and are big supporters of peace. I am proud to be Gypsy.

Life for Gypsies in Israel is different today than life in my parents' and their parents' generations. My father reminisced about the good old days. It was a difficult life then, but they were proud of their culture and led simple lives. They never wanted more than they had and were always sharing. They lived an amazing old-style simple life in Jerusalem.

The older generation laughs at us and thinks we are close-minded and cannot see the beautiful side of life in this discriminated community. Their generation was built on being proud, and it is not the case today. Day by day, they left tomorrow for tomorrow, believing only God knows what is tomorrow. Many people thought they were crazy and irresponsible, just taking things easy. Now I look at how people rush around in this world. I think they should come and learn to slow down their lives.

I look at the Domari Center and the challenges we face to keep our work going. Then I see unique signs with happy kids, young men opening their hands for help, and lovely women around us. I believe it is not a coincidence. It is a beautiful song from God and makes this life surrounded by hope.

At the end of 2012, I thought of many things. It had been the year I said goodbye to people close to my heart—my father and my oldest brother. Not long after, my brother's daughter Dania broke her hand and had to have surgery. She came to the center to have a change as she recovered. She was happy and tried to write with her arm. It made me smile. I miss my father and my brother Shaker, but I know he would be proud of his daughter.

The year had been happy and sad with a threat of war, and I remembered the real friends who make a difference in my life. As the new year began, I hoped for more rest and more joy and peace to all, including friends all around the world.

I still dream in Jerusalem. Sometimes, I don't know if I must keep dreaming. Sometimes I wish to see the light at the end of the tunnel. Still, I dream of preserving the Domari language and handicrafts. I dream of educating children who will grow up to meet their goals. I dream of women who use their talents to provide for themselves and their families I dream of men who overcome their embarrassment at their illiteracy and learn to read and write. I dream that Gypsies will take pride in their own culture and gain respect from the rest of the world.

In spite of the difficulties, the old feeling of contentment that I felt as a child sitting outside the wall looking over to the Mount of Olives remains with me today. My trust in God is so high with hopes for more doors to open. The Domari Center will live! I feel I am a princess. Thank God. Every day I have everything a human can have.

AMOUN'S WORDS OF WISDOM

Friends and Family

- Sometimes being honest will not bring a lot of people around you, but it will always get the right ones.
- My father's saying before I went to work was, "Just remember there are always people who love you and wait to see you back in the evening."
- Don't let anyone convince you there is a reason he stays away from you. A true friend will find hundreds of ways to reach you.
- There are friends like food. You need them all the time. There are friends like medicine. You need them when you are sick. And there are friends like a disease. You don't need them at all.
- They say those who live far from the eyes, live far from the heart. That's something I never believe because there are many who live far, but they still live very close to our hearts.
- To be rich or poor doesn't matter. What matters is your history and what your history is telling you. I love the Domari history and am proud of the past they lived.
- I am so proud of my heart that cries and smiles, is sad and happy, goes up and down, but it still works and is open for others.
- I love when the kids at the center call me "Aunt Amoun." That means they want something—very smart kids I have around me.
- I believe those who stick by your side through your worst time deserve to be with you through your best time.
- Sometimes I have complained about the painful moments when I had been hurt because I was a Gypsy. Now I think I was lucky and appreciate what God was giving me all these years.
- Too many chefs in the kitchen make the food burn. You know what will happen to that food.

Enemies

- I laugh at my system of life and how I go on believing in people who make many promises even though many times I am disappointed.
- Remember if someone hits you in the back that you are still in front and will be the first to reach the top.

- There are people in our lives like stones. What we need to do is push them aside and continue on our way.
- If you want to live in balance, get rid of those who find you if they need you, but you can never find them when you need them.
- My Grandmother told my dad, "There will be many stones you find in your way, but the clever way is to collect them and build from them a road to walk on."

Forgiveness

- The first step for a better life is forgiveness. It's the best medicine.
- Live with forgiveness. It makes you always feel rich.
- I always try to forgive others who have hurt me—not because they deserve forgiveness, but because I deserve peace inside me.
- I do believe sometimes we forgive people we love simply because we still want them in our lives.

Self-confidence

- Always remember that you are unique and worthy to be loved.
- The only true wisdom is in knowing you know nothing. That will make your life easier.
- A good life is when you have nothing more you need. Smile often and dream big. Laugh as much as you can. It's good for your face and healthy for your body.
- Sometimes I have lost my way and found myself in the middle of nowhere, but I am glad that God showed me the way to find myself.
- Always stay true to yourself, because there are few people who will always be true to you!
- I love the Center when it looks full of people, but I love it even more when it is quiet. Then I can have the cup of coffee and the piece of chocolate that I really need.
- Morning never changes. Every day comes with more beautiful things. You need to discover it.
- Be kind to everyone, including yourself.
- When we were kids, we put water on our faces to look like tears. Now we put water on our faces to hide our tears.
- Always try to give and listen to others, but don't lose your own voice.

Jerusalem

- What I don't like in Jerusalem is our strange weather. Dust. Hot. Cold. Wind. I just don't understand our weather any more.
- I don't live in a palace, but I am glad with this Old City of Jerusalem inside the Wall of Jerusalem. What do I seek more? I love my city!
- Jerusalem spirit on Friday is different than any other day of the week. It's God's line to humans to tell us it's the day to rest. When you walk around the City, you see all kinds of faces, a good sign that this is family day. What is amazing is that God always makes us fresh and heals us to start a new week.

The Future

- Never lose hope. You don't know what tomorrow may bring. God always gives a second chance. There will always be tomorrow.
- Sometimes we don't see the whole staircase before us. We just need to take that first step.
- Something beautiful for the future deserves patience. That's what I see in the kids at the Domari Center. They are the future.
- My grandmother said, "Live today and leave tomorrow for God, so let's open our hearts and wish a day full of blessing to everyone around us."
- When you remember your history, it is proof that you have lived.
- Love is like life. No path is clear. No step is easy!
- Two things can destroy a person. One is to be busy with the past. The other is to be busy watching what other people are doing. We should make a way from the past to the future and keep on.
- You can't always get what you wish for, but you can always try just to be a little closer to what you want.
- Keep going each step. It may get harder and harder, but you must not stop. The view at the top is great and beautiful.
- I say these words to myself with a short prayer when I feel I have lost my way and need to see the light in the tunnel I am going through, "Amoun, always try to keep your life simple and avoid the crazy life around you. Put your concerns and worries before God."
- A wise person makes a boat that crosses the river rather than building walls around himself to be protected from flooding.
- Yesterday is yesterday, and today is today. When I find rocks in my way, I should collect these rocks and build me a wall to cross the world.

Hopes and Dreams

- To wish for something is always possible, but it is not always possible to have what you wish for.
- Life is like onions. Some of them make us cry, and some of them don't make us cry. Jerusalem is a sweet onion all the time.
- We are sometimes afraid of one small step to take in our life. We live in our daily routine and forget this step can change our life forever. We should believe we have nothing to lose to try.
- When we close our eyes to pray, to cry, to dream, the most beautiful things in life are not seen but are the feelings found in our own hearts.
- I always try to keep smiling, not because everything is great and perfect in my life, but to give a sign to everyone around me that I appreciate what I have right now in my hands. I keep saying better days are coming in God's will.

God

- When people close one door, God opens ten others.
- If people forget us, still be happy. There will be a door open. It's God's door.
- Those who don't thank people, don't thank God.
- God is beauty, and he created us in beauty. If you look through those eyes, you will see the world in beauty.
- I never say God is in my heart. I say I am in God's heart.
- Nobody has a perfect life. Everybody has their own problems, but if we deal with them in God's love, we will find a perfect way.
- I love the moments when I talk to God to fill my batteries. Believe me, to work with Gypsies, you need long-term batteries.
- When I am poor financially, I feel I am rich in God's eyes. When people treat me with racism and ignore me, I face that with love and forgiveness. I am not trying to be holy, but trying to be human and pass on love and forgiveness as I was raised in the Family Sleem.

ACKNOWLEDGEMENTS

There are many friends who have passed through my life from my child-hood until this time when I am getting older. These people left so much in my life. I remember them with many small details. These are people that I love and care about until this very moment. I thank these people as well as organizations who have encouraged me in my personal goals and dreams, helped establish and support the Domari Center, and assisted in the publication of this book.

Organizations

Diakonie: Heide Kautt (sent volunteers for one year from Germany)
Dom Research Center
Domari Society Board (members of the Domari community)
Global Fund for Women (supports the women's program)
Jerusalem College (sends volunteers from USA)
Kinderpostzegeles Holland (an organization that supports children's tutoring programs)
Notre Dame College (has cooperated with the Domari Center for many years for vocational training classes)
Sunbula Jerusalem (supports women's handicraft)

Individuals

Many of these individuals have helped the center by showing up in times when we needed them, even though they work and have jobs of their own.

Abigail Wood
Anat Hoffman (the head of the Domari Society Board)
Anna, Andrea, Lena (volunteers)
Anneke de Kok (promoting Gypsies in Holland)
Ariela Marshall (volunteer)
Calvary Chapel and Pastor Dwight Douville (Wisconsin, USA)
Caral Miles has a kind heart for the Gypsy people.
Chef Abed Al-Karim Shamaseh (physically support, involved in women-catering)

Group of volunteers at the Domari Society Community Center.

Chef Azam Salbhab (physically support, involved in women-catering)

Coby and VeldhyZen (promoting Gypsies in Holland)

Corrie van Manen (promoting Gypsies in Holland)

Dafnah Strauss has supported the Domari Center for all these years.

Dina Zreineh (accounting)

Dina Feldman (supporter for Domari)

Donna Rathke (good friend of the Domari and good supporter for many
    years)

Elin Elkouby (tour guide, promotion in Norway)

Father Jean Michael de Tarragon from the Ecole Biblique

Francis Tams (Domari Society Accountant)

Hana Nasseredin (supported the center physically)

Jan Poortman (promoting Gypsies in Holland)

Jan van der Graaf (promoting Gypsies in Holland)

Joel Soffin (helped get computers for kids)

Johanne Bergkuist (support to get connection with Norwegian Gypsies)

Kamelia Alami (great supporter for the Domari)

Kathleen Hoffart

Linda Abu GhaZaleh (supporting women handicrafts)

Louann Luck (friend and supporter of the Domari)

Lynette & Michael Stewart (volunteers)

Marina (good friend)

Mia Kainulanen (very good friend from Finnland)

Michael Yates (volunteer)
Omri Kabiri (lawyer)
Pandora Letitia (friend of the Domari)
Petra van der Zande (great supporter of the Domair, since we met)
Rima Shehadeh (support physically)
Ron Swanson (helping the Domari also by giving hope and strength)
Samuel Vigardt (promoting Gypsies in Norway)
Shirabe Yamada (gave the center a great push for handicrafts)
Tamara (supporter of Domari)
Taylor Luck (good friend of the Domari)
Tiina Timonen (good friend of Domari society and supporter of the Dom)
Tony Shiloh (teaching children English)
Willemina and Jan den Dikken (promoting Gypsies in Holland)

This Book Publication

Allen and Verr Dean Williams, who have been like a brother and sister to me, believed I had a good story and helped make connections so this book could happen. Thank you to Virginia McGee Butler for being the wordsmith who helped me put my narrative in order.

Amoun Sleem and Virginia McGee Butler working on Amoun's book in Mississippi, 2013.

CPSIA information can be obtained at www.ICGtesting.com
Printed in the USA
LVOW04s1326260515

439931LV00023B/383/P

9 781938 514500